j746.46   Bogen, Constance.
B   A beginner's book of patchwork,
           applique, and quilting. New York,
           Dodd, Mead [1974]
              159 p. illus. 25 cm.

MOUNT CLEMENS PUBLIC LIBRARY

        1. Patchwork. 2. Quilting. 3.
     Applique. I. Title.
TT835.B55   746.4'6
ISBN 0-396-06863-4   73-11989
                                              MARC
Library of Congress
04331   533106   © THE BAKER & TAYLOR CO.   5195

A BEGINNER'S BOOK
OF
PATCHWORK,
APPLIQUE,
AND
QUILTING

A BEGINNER'S BOOK
OF
PATCHWORK,
APPLIQUE,
AND
QUILTING

Constance Bogen

Illustrated with diagrams and photographs

DODD, MEAD & COMPANY · NEW YORK

CONTENTS

A beautiful applique and embroidered quilt made in the early nineteenth century. The central panel, showing scenes of farm life, is surrounded by a flower border. (*The Metropolitan Museum of Art, Gift of Catherine E. Cotheal, 1938.*)

INTRODUCTION

Patchwork, applique, and quilting are crafts which are enjoying a revival of interest. Not only are the traditional bed quilts becoming more popular, but also many other articles which can be pieced, appliqued and quilted, such as clothing, stuffed animals, tablecloths, and innumerable other items.

Did you ever think of a quilt as being beautiful enough to be considered a work of art? If your answer is yes, then you agree with many quilt collectors, craftswomen, and even museums. Quilts are not only practical, but they are cherished by many people who see them not only as a fireside craft, but as a fine art. Most museums around the country show quilts as an important part of their textile collections. Go to see them, and you will be very impressed with their color, charm, and workmanship.

The designs on the quilts need not be elaborate at all. In fact, motifs on most quilts are very simple—flowers, geometrical shapes—but they can look like beautiful paintings in themselves. They are colorful, balanced in design, well scaled, and carefully made.

Examples of quilted clothing have been shown in ancient statuary— some 3,000 years old. Even quilted rugs, from approximately the second century, show this needlecraft as a finely developed art. Quilted clothing, particularly thick military jackets worn under armor, was used from the time of the Crusades into the sixteenth century. In the eighteenth century, fashionable European women enjoyed the warmth and beauty of quilted silk petticoats and quilted coverlets.

As the necessity for quilts grew, especially in European countries with bitter winters, the quilting art became more refined and the designs more

One quilt can be made by many helping hands. Here, a group of women at a modern quilting bee are constructing a Wedding Ring pattern. (Courtesy of Appalachian Fireside Crafts Organized by Save the Children Federation. Photograph by Ken Heyman.)

imaginative. The French needlewoman introduced applique—the sewing on of pieces to a background fabric—to quilts, and the Italians devised Trapunto—a quilting technique that outlines a design which is later stuffed to make it a three-dimensional form. The invention of the quilting frame, which holds the quilt in place while it is being sewn together, added to the ease of sewing the three layers of fabric together.

In America, colonial women revived quilting and made it as much a part of the home life as the hearth. The hard life of the colonists inspired women with ingenuity. Odd scraps of fabric were salvaged and saved and, out of necessity, the patchwork quilt was born. Quilting bees became an important part of the community life, with many women simultaneously quilting the many blocks of a quilt. Handed-down European motifs were used, but imagination soon gave way to many of the traditional American designs that are still used today.

Quilting, patchwork, and applique are the kinds of crafts that easily adapt to other forms than making a bed quilt. Appliques can be put on jackets, purses, place mats, or any fabric object you wish to decorate. Patchwork can be made and used for clothing, stuffed toys, aprons, table-

A whimsical lion is made with patched squares in various patterns. His head is framed in wool yarn fringe and his face is embroidered. (*Courtesy of Appalachian Spring.*)

Three hand-pieced pillows, each with a single flower motif. Each pillow is quilted. The pattern on the left is Ohio Rose, the center one is Dollie's Star, and on the right, Dresden Plate. *(Courtesy of Appalachian Fireside Crafts Organized by Save the Children Federation.)*

cloths, and dolls. All you need to do is piece together a length of patchwork fabric, then cut out what you want to make from it. Quilting techniques can be applied to fabric purses, skirts, jackets, potholders, pillows, and toys.

You'll discover the fun of quilting, applique, and patchwork and its many applications as you learn to master these traditional crafts. Here's how.

1

SOME BASICS

If you have been fortunate enough to inherit an old quilt you were probably awed by the workmanship. Your first thought, no doubt, was that such a project couldn't be attempted. But this is far from true. Aside from planning your design, and cutting accurate pieces, all that is necessary to know are a few simple stitches. Piecing a quilt is a relatively easy procedure that asks only for your time and patience. Practice is all it takes to master the stitching, even for the actual quilting. Your design for a quilt can come from innumerable patterns which have been carried down through generations, or you can make up your own.

However, there are a few terms which you should be familiar with before you begin.

Patchwork consists of patched-together pieces of fabric in geometrical shapes—hexagons, squares, triangles, or curves. These are sewn together to make the particular pattern which you have decided on for your design.

The pleasure of patchworking is creating something new and exciting from just fabric scraps. As with colonial women, you can save pieces of fabric from old clothes, or you can buy new materials for your projects. The quilts of the colonial women were greatly prized by those who made them and, of course, by those lucky ones who received them.

Patchwork can be large pieces of fabric or small pieces. It is interesting to note that patchwork seems to know no bounds as far as just how many pieces may be used for a quilt top. A crafts*man* in Illinois actually sewed a patchwork quilt top together using 63,000 pieces!

Patchwork is easy to do. All it takes is the ability to baste two pieces of fabric together and sew a seam securely and straight. Sewing by machine

Detail of a nineteenth-century quilt in blue and white. The pattern is a variation of Jacob's Ladder. (*Courtesy of America Hurrah.*)

makes the work go faster, but hand sewing will give you a great sense of pride in accomplished needlework.

Applique is simply a small piece or pieces of shaped fabric attached to a larger background fabric with a running, hemming, or embroidery stitch.

We've all seen commercial appliques in notion stores—machine-made floral, alphabet, and animal shapes edged in a close-set zigzag stitch. The familiar stripes on a soldier's sleeve and the sew-on ecology symbol are also appliques.

Quilting itself is quite simple. It is the sewing together of three layers—the top, the middle or filling layer, and the bottom lining—with a short running stitch. Usually a quilting pattern is designed so that it will be decorative when sewn. This design is marked on the article before the quilting is done, so that it will be uniform throughout the work.

If you are planning to make a quilt, the top can be either appliqued or pieced, or a combination of both. It will usually be made up of individual

A velvet wall hanging features an abstract stuffed applique design in bright colors and patterns. Made by Virginia Davis.

squares known as *blocks*. The pattern or design can be repeated on each block or sometimes alternated with plain blocks. The number of blocks you make depends on how large the quilt is to be. Sewing together a particular number of blocks will form the top of the quilt in the motif you have chosen. Some quilt tops are made of one piece of fabric with an over-all design appliqued on it. A variety of choices are open to you in planning a quilt—from design, color scheme, fabrics, and techniques.

As with a puzzle, every piece of patchwork and applique must fit perfectly in place, and this is accomplished by cutting accurate pieces. This is the most important thing to remember. When the pieces are cut accurately, then there will be no problem assembling the parts to form your design.

Because today's fabrics are so easy to care for and rarely fade drastically or shrink beyond further use—the way they used to when these crafts began—what will concern you most is choosing the prints you like in terms of what you are making. Pieced and appliqued bed quilts can be made from

13

The Cat quilt is a nineteenth-century quilt done in green, red, and white. It's an unusual example, with its cat shapes encircling the central motif. (*Courtesy of America Hurrah.*)

cotton, muslin, Dacron/cotton mixtures, calico, or any combination of these. When you gain the skill in these crafts—after you do the practice pieces in the chapters on patchwork and applique—you will want to try harder to manage fabrics like velvet, satin, or even a high-pile cloth. But cotton or cotton/Dacron mixtures are the best to learn with.

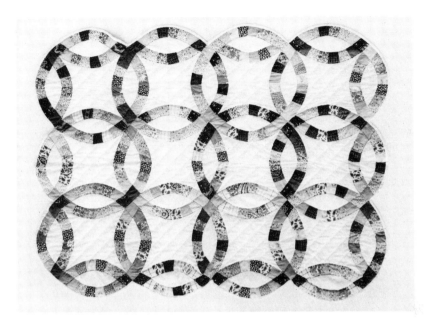

Double Wedding Ring makes an unusual and striking pattern. It's constructed of small patches pieced together in a circle and placing them so they look interlocked. Note that the outer edge of the quilt keeps the rounded form of the circles. (*Courtesy of Appalachian Spring.*)

Stitches

There are several basic stitches which are used in patchwork, applique, and quilting.

The *Running Stitch* (Fig. 1) is accomplished with a single in-and-out motion. By holding the needle at an angle, you can take three or four

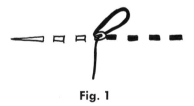

Fig. 1

small stitches at once before you pull the needle through the fabric. This stitch is used for sewing together two pieces of patchwork, sewing appliques

15

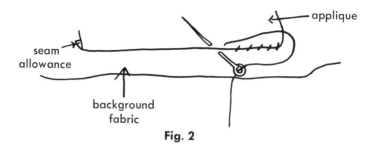

Fig. 2

to background fabric, and also for sewing together the three pieces of your quilted object.

The *Hemming Stitch* (Fig. 2) is a simple stitch that's made by sewing from right to left, with the tip of the needle merely catching the very edge of the applique. For the second step, the needle is brought down into the background fabric, then, keeping the needle at an angle, brought back up through the edge of the applique.

Fig. 3A   **Fig. 3B**

The *Backstitch* (Figs. 3A and 3B) can also be used to join two pieces of patchwork. The backstitch begins by knotting the thread and coming up through the fabric from below. Take a *short* stitch to the right and in one motion go into the fabric and come out a short stitch to the left of where you started, as in Fig. 3A.

The second step is to go back into the left end of the first stitch you made and, again, coming out a short stitch away to the left, as in Fig. 3B.

The *Back-Lock Stitch* (Fig. 4) is used for ending a row of running or

Fig. 4

hemming stitches. By going over the last stitch, the thread makes a secure lock so the other stitches don't come loose. This same stitch is used in quilting, except that when quilting, both the first and last stitch will be back-locked, so there will be no knots at all. When you take the last stitch, go back into the same beginning and ending of the stitch as shown. Pull the thread, and snip.

In doing any stitch, it is important to remember to keep the line of stitches as straight as you can, so that the seams will be straight and lie flat when they are pressed.

Using a Template

When doing patchwork or applique for a quilt top, the patterns should be uniform throughout all the blocks making up the top. For this, it is necessary to have the same shape and size of the pieces throughout. To make each applique and patchwork piece the same, a template is made.

A *Template* is a cardboard or oaktag pattern that is cut in the shape that you want to use again and again—a triangle, a square, an applique flower, or a quilting design. A cardboard pattern works better when using the same repeated shape because cardboard is sturdier than paper and never needs to be pinned to the fabric like a paper pattern. When you make and use a template, you will be tracing around it, not weakening it by pinning.

To make a template, first do an original drawing—a simple shape to begin with—or, trace out one of the patterns in this book on a piece of paper. Tracing paper or typing paper is fine. IMPORTANT TO REMEMBER: Always include a ¼″ seam allowance when cutting a template for applique and patchwork. (It is not necessary for your quilting design.) In piecing together fabric, a seam of ¼″ is always left, and on appliques ¼″ is left to turn under for a hem. If you cut the shape in the exact size you want without including the seam allowance, the pieces will come out smaller after they have been seamed together or appliqued. If you are making an applique with felt, the hem allowance is not needed, because felt does not unravel and thus does not need to be turned under at the edges.

Here's how to measure for a seam allowance. Draw the shape you have decided on. For example, let's use an oval (Fig. 5).

Now, take a ruler and begin to measure ¼″ around the shape, leaving

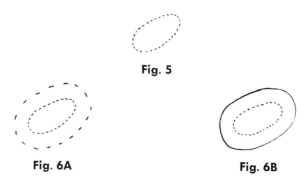

Fig. 5

Fig. 6A   **Fig. 6B**

about ¼" between pencil marks. Measure completely around the shape (Fig. 6A). Connect the dots as shown in Fig. 6B. When you make your template, you'll be cutting around the outside line, which will provide for the seam allowance.

Now that you have the shape desired, including the seam allowance, a template can be made from your paper drawing. With two dabs of glue (be sure that the glue isn't lumpy or drenching the paper), press the paper shape to the piece of cardboard or oaktag. Trace around the paper shape, carefully, with a soft pencil or fine-lined ink marker. Cut out the cardboard shape, and either lift off the paper pattern or leave it on if you prefer. This is the finished template.

If you are cutting out geometrical shapes like squares, equal-sided triangles, circles, or ovals, two can be cut at once by folding the fabric with the wrong sides together (Fig. 7).

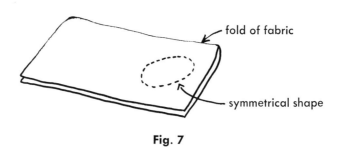

fold of fabric

symmetrical shape

Fig. 7

When cutting out asymmetrical shapes like free-form flowers, animals, or odd-shaped pieces, do *not* place the template on a folded fabric. Rather, stack the fabric right side up. If you cut odd-shaped pieces on folded fabric with the right sides together, the resulting pieces will be the reverse, or mirror image. Stack the fabric as in Fig. 8.

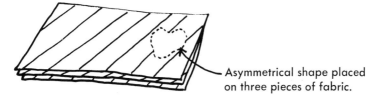

Asymmetrical shape placed on three pieces of fabric.

The right side of each piece of fabric is face up.

Fig. 8

To begin cutting your pieces follow these steps (Fig. 9):

1. Hold the template down on the fabric with your left hand, and with your right, trace around the shape with a pencil.

2. Place two or three pins inside the traced shape before you begin cutting. This insures that the fabric won't move and your cutting will be the same through both layers of the fabric.

3. Cut out the shape.

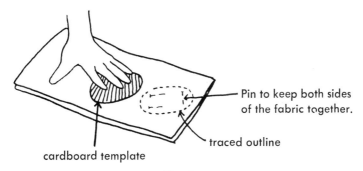

Pin to keep both sides of the fabric together.

traced outline

cardboard template

Fig. 9

Organizing Pieces and Appliques

When a quilt has many different patterns and shapes, all the many pieces can wind up in a very confused jumble unless they're kept in order. The way to keep the parts so they can be at a finger's touch is to string each group of the same pattern together as shown in Fig. 10. Knot a thread and then pull it through the entire group of pieces. Don't knot the other end and you'll be able to just lift off the pieces as you need them.

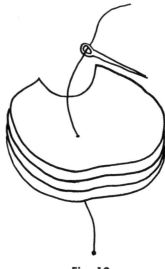

Fig. 10

Now that we have covered some of the basic steps you will have to follow in doing these crafts, you should be ready to begin.

2

PATCHWORK

When you do patchwork, you will be piecing together two pieces of fabric which will then be joined to other patched pieces. Patchwork quilts are made of blocks sewn together, each block consisting of several pieces sewn together. Each block is usually made up of the same number of pieces, cut in the same way to form a design, and then the blocks are stitched together.

While the design or pattern—the shape of the pieces and the way they are stitched together—may be repeated for each block, the type and pattern

Left: A handsome pillow worked in blocks of three rectangles sewn vertically and horizontally to make a pattern called Roman Stripe. (*Courtesy of Appalachian Spring.*) Right: A nineteenth-century embroidered velvet and silk section of a crazy quilt, with Grandmother's Fan in opposite corners. (*Courtesy of America Hurrah.*)

of the fabric may vary. Solid colors, prints, flowered fabrics, even stripes can be used. Traditional patterns may call for solid colors and prints in particular shapes and in particular positions, but you can also make up your own pattern or design, using fabric pieces of your own choosing.

There is also "crazy quilt" patchwork in which pieces of varying sizes and shapes are fitted and stitched together, with no special pattern followed. Solid colors and prints are used—whatever happens to strike one's fancy or happens to be on hand—and the whole is a riot of gay colors.

Patchwork pieces for traditional quilt designs are made up of pieces of fabrics cut in squares, triangles, diamonds, or rectangles. The sizes will vary according to the pattern you have selected to follow, but with these geometrical shapes you have an infinite variety of designs. Sewing the

One of the more colorful patchwork designs is Grandmother's Flower Garden, done here on a full-sized quilt. (Courtesy of Heirloom Crafts.)

22

pieces together is done with a short running stitch, backstitched on both ends so that the seams will be secure.

There are a few essential rules for doing patchwork:

1. Cut the patches accurately. Perfect fit for all your pieces should be your goal, so take time and cut with care.

2. Keep all the seams straight and even and allow the same seam allowance throughout, usually ¼", so that all the pieces will fit together accurately.

3. Always press the seams open after you join the pieces. This gives a nice, smooth finished appearance to your seaming.

Patchwork Squares

Always be sure, when you sew squares together, that the right sides of the fabric are face-to-face (Fig. 1). If you are sewing by machine, pin the squares together, keeping the pins horizontal. Be sure to leave your ¼" seam allowance. You can sew right over the pins. If your machine doesn't sew over pins easily, then baste the squares with a long stitch. Be sure that the side you are sewing is corner to corner, so that the squares

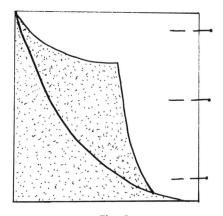

Fig. 1

come out evenly. If you sew by hand, use a small, evenly spaced running stitch. Or, if your prefer, the backstitch can be used.

When the two squares are sewn together, they should look like Fig. 2.

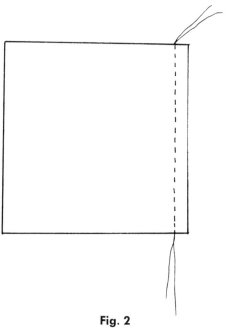

Fig. 2

Open up the squares, and press down the seam allowance with a moderately hot iron. The open squares look like Fig. 3.

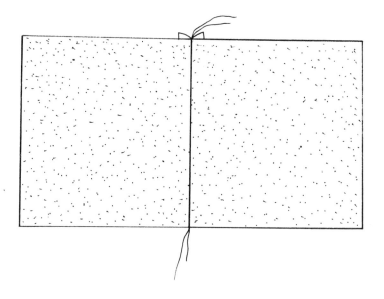

Fig. 3

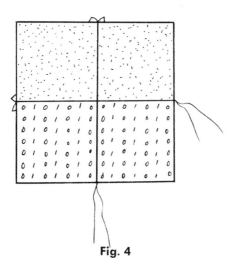

Fig. 4

When sewing squares, always work across a row, finishing it completely before you add any other squares. Fig. 4 shows *two* rows of squares already sewn together. The first row consists of two squares with a stippled pattern. These two squares were sewn together, then put aside. The second row is a dot and slash pattern made up of two squares also. These two squares were sewn together. Then, the two rows were sewn to each other, matching the seam allowances to make sure that all the squares were the same size after they were sewn together

One of the mistakes that's made when doing patchwork is to try to squeeze and fit a square into an available spot, as in Fig. 5. This makes for

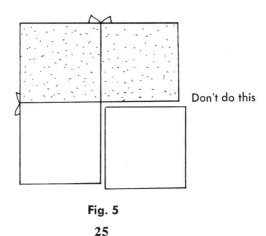

Don't do this

Fig. 5

difficulty since it will be hard to get the two sides that need to be sewn to the others sewn in evenly. Often, a little hole results where the seams meet.

So, if you are making a patchwork pattern that is five rows wide and five rows long, as in Fig. 6, here's how to sew it correctly.

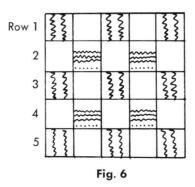

Fig. 6

1. Sew the five squares together that make up the first row, as in Fig. 7.

2. Sew the five squares together that make up the second row, as in Fig. 8.

3. Match the seam allowances and sew Row One to Row Two, as shown in Fig. 9.

4. Continue down the patchwork pattern. First *complete* each row, then sew it to the preceding row.

The Nine-Patch is one of the easiest patchwork patterns to accomplish. It's three squares wide and three squares long. What makes the Nine-Patch

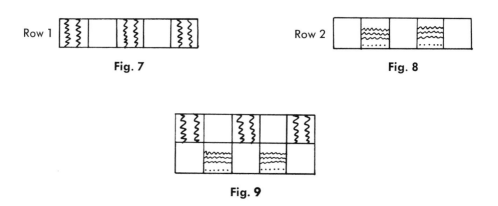

Fig. 7

Fig. 8

Fig. 9

26

exciting is its many variations—the patterns of fabric and how they are sewn together is what makes it *more* than just nine squares.

Nine-Patch with an Applique Number 9

Trace out the four-inch square (Fig 10), make a paper pattern, then a template. Cut out nine four-inch squares—four in a solid fabric, five in a patterned fabric The seam allowance has been provided for in the pattern, so you won't have to measure for it. Trace out the pattern for the number 9 (Fig. 11) on a piece of tracing paper or typing paper. Lay the pattern on a piece of felt, trace around it, and cut it out.

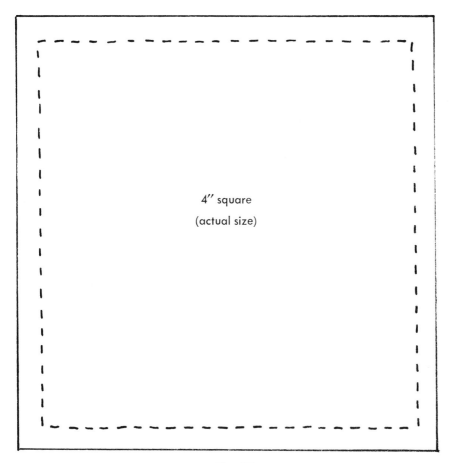

4″ square

(actual size)

Fig. 10

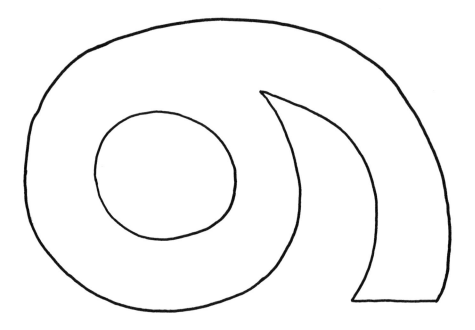

Fig. 11

To sew the squares together for the classic Nine-Patch:

ROW ONE: Sew together one patterned square, one solid colored square, and one patterned square. Put the completed row aside.

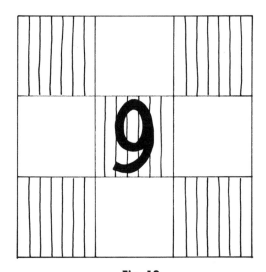

Fig. 12

ROW TWO: Sew together one solid, one patterned, and one solid square. Sew Row One to Row Two, matching seam allowances.

ROW THREE: Sew together one patterned, one solid, and one patterned square. Sew Row Three to Row Two, matching seam allowances. Press the seam allowances open.

Now, place the number 9 in the center square. Pin, then baste in place. Sew it to the center square with a short running stitch (Fig. 12).

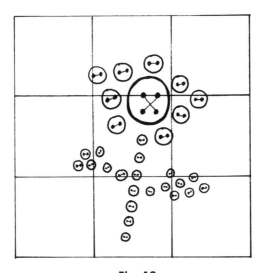

Fig. 13

Nine-Patch with Button Motif

Besides appliqueing a Nine-Patch, you can use buttons of varying sizes to "draw" a design. Tiny shirt buttons make the stem and leaves, and medium and large buttons construct the flower (Fig. 13). As with fabric scraps, odd-size and odd-number buttons taken from no longer worn clothes can always be put to new and imaginative use with patchwork.

Use the four-inch square pattern to make this Nine-Patch. Cut nine squares from the same fabric—either solid or patterned. Sew them together row by row, then sew the rows together. Press the seams. Follow the diagram in Fig. 13 to see where and how many buttons are to be placed in each square.

29

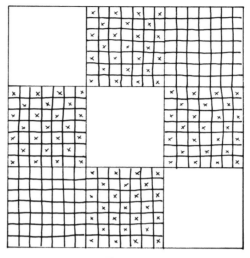

Fig. 14

Nine-Patch with Diagonal Light Squares

Use the pattern for the four-inch square for this variation. Cut nine squares in this scheme: Three very light patterned or solid colored squares, four dark colored squares, and two medium-toned squares. This is a classic patchwork pattern made with the lightest tone fabric running in the diagonal from left to right (Fig 14).

ROW ONE: Sew one light square, one dark square, and one medium square together. Set aside.

ROW TWO: Sew one dark, one light, and another dark square together. Sew Row Two to Row One.

ROW THREE: Sew one medium, one dark, and one light square together. Sew Row Three to Row Two. Press seams.

Appliqued Nine-Patch

Use the four-inch square pattern (Fig. 10), make a template, and cut nine squares of the same colored fabric. Before you start sewing the squares together, mark the center of seven squares with a pencil. Measure a one-inch square (plus the ¼″ seam allowance all around), and make a template for it. Cut seven one-inch squares in a contrasting colored fabric. Before

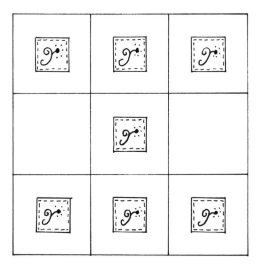

Fig. 15

you baste down the seam allowance on the one-inch squares, mark the center of each one.

ROW ONE: Sew three four-inch squares together. Set aside.

ROW TWO: Sew three more four-inch squares together. Sew Row Two to Row One.

ROW THREE: Sew the last three four-inch squares together. Sew Row Three to Row Two.

Baste down the ¼″ seam allowance all around on each of the seven one-inch applique squares.

Put the center point of the applique squares on the center point of the seven four-inch patchwork squares, as shown in Fig. 15. Pin, then baste. Sew the applique squares to the patches with a short running stitch in a contrasting colored thread.

Scottie

A little Scottie appears from among the many squares (Fig. 16). He's constructed from two-inch squares sewn together in two contrasting colors. Use the pattern for the two-inch square (Fig. 17), make a template, and cut the following: 35 squares in a dark colored fabric for the Scottie and 65 squares in a light colored fabric for the background. His collar is a

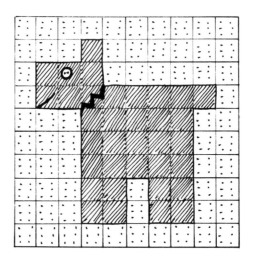

Fig. 16

short piece of rickrack, and his eye is a large two-hole coat button. The mouth is backstitched on with embroidery thread.

ROW ONE: Sew ten light squares together. Set aside.

ROW TWO: Sew three light, one dark, six light squares together. Sew Row Two to Row One.

ROW THREE: Sew one light, three dark, six light squares together. Sew Row Three to Row Two.

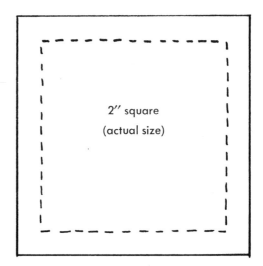

2″ square
(actual size)

Fig. 17

ROW FOUR: One light, eight dark, one light square sewn together. Sew Row Four to Row Three.

ROW FIVE: Three light, five dark, two light squares sewn together. Sew Row Five to Row Four.

ROW SIX: Three light, five dark, two light squares sewn together. Sew Row Six to Row Five.

ROW SEVEN: Three light, five dark, two light squares sewn together. Sew Row Seven to Row Six.

ROW EIGHT: Three light, two dark, one light, two dark, two light squares sewn together. Sew Row Eight to Row Seven.

ROW NINE: Three light, two dark, one light, two dark, two light squares sewn together. Sew Row Nine to Row Eight.

ROW TEN: Ten light squares sewn together. Sew Row Ten to Row Nine.

Cut a piece of rickrack to fit diagonally on the third dark square of the fourth row. Sew down with a running stitch.

Sew a large button approximately in the center of the second dark square of the third row.

Sew a smile on the Scottie with embroidery thread in a constrasting color. His mouth goes on the first dark square in the fourth row.

Patchwork Triangles

The fun of sewing many rows of triangles together is the enormous variation in design that you can get with them. The kind of design depends on how the triangles are sewn to each other. Each triangle is exactly half a square, so when two triangles of the same size are sewn together on the longest side, they will form a complete square.

Using the pattern for the four-inch triangle (Fig. 18), make a template of the triangle and cut out several sample triangles.

Take two triangles and place the right sides together, as in Fig. 19, and pin along the long side. This is the side that will be sewn. Sew along the ¼" seam allowance, as in Fig. 20.

Now open up the sewn triangles and press the seam open. The seam allowance will overlap the corners of the square that's just been made. Clip off the four overlapping pieces as indicated by the arrows in Fig. 21.

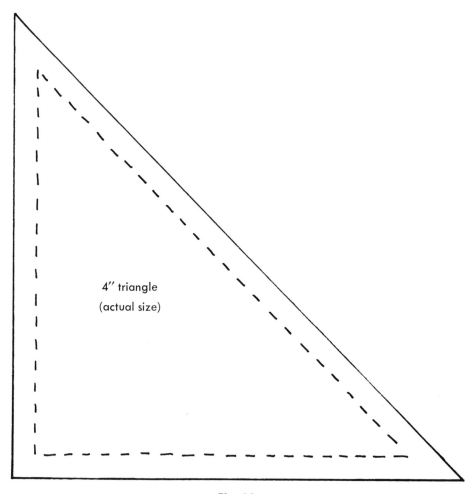

4″ triangle
(actual size)

Fig. 18

In Fig. 22, four triangles of two different fabrics—a print and a solid—have been joined to achieve a zigzag effect. If the square on the right is turned around, so it's sewn print-to-print, the result is a large inverted V shape, as in Fig. 23. Sew four squares together, each with the print triangles edge to edge, and a large diamond appears, as in Fig. 24. Position the print triangles in each square, as in Fig. 25, and the resulting form is a pinwheel, which is a variation of a traditional patchwork pattern called the Double T.

Combining triangle-made squares with one-piece squares increases patchwork possibilities. Treat the triangle-made square like a one-piece

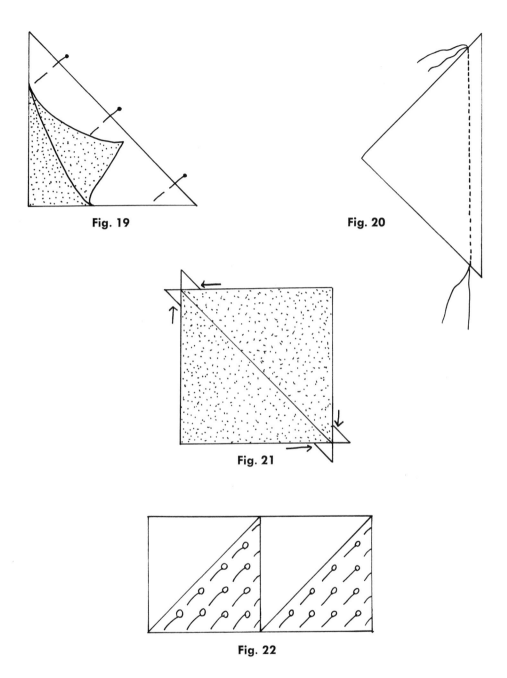

Fig. 19

Fig. 20

Fig. 21

Fig. 22

square. Cut out a four-inch square, pin it right side down to the triangle-made square. Sew together with a ¼″ seam allowance. Open it up and it will look like Fig. 26. You'll notice that the seam line of the triangle-made

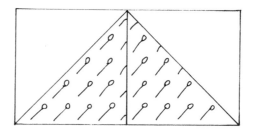

Fig. 23

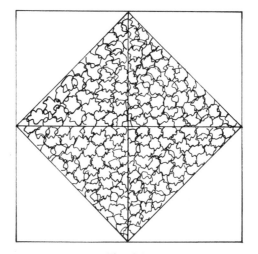

Fig. 24

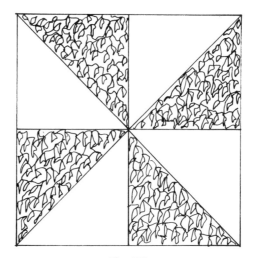

Fig. 25

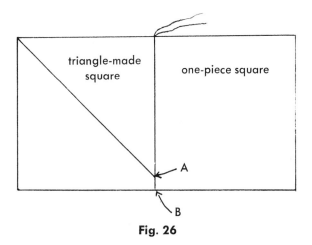

triangle-made
square

one-piece square

A

B

Fig. 26

square *does not* fall into the exact corner. Measuring the space between A and B will show that it is ¼″. This disappears when you sew a second row

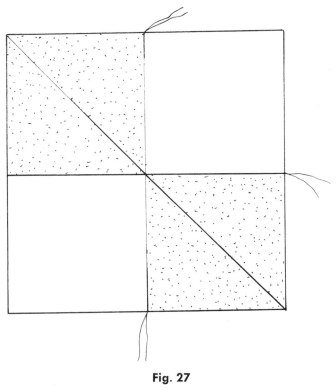

Fig. 27

One of the possibilities for using your own patchwork fabric is then cutting out a pattern for a stuffed toy. Here, a charming hippo with hat and tie. *(Courtesy of Appalachian Spring.)*

to this row. Fig. 27 shows two rows of triangle-made squares combined with one-piece squares.

The number of patchwork creations from squares and triangles is probably infinite. The larger the number of triangles and squares used to form a design, the greater and more imaginative they can be. Since the beauty of patchwork is piecing many prints and solids together to get sometimes very elaborate designs, experimenting with a dozen squares and a dozen triangle-made squares will inspire new and personal creations.

Remember that *two* triangles will make up *one* square, and that four or more squares (whether made from triangles or just a solid square) will make up one block.

Here are some patterns to experiment with:

Fig. 28 is made by positioning all the light triangles edge to edge, so that they form a large diamond. A small center square in the same printed fabric as the outside triangles has been appliqued to the center.

Fig. 29 combines squares and triangles, with a dark patterned fabric used only for the outside triangles.

Fig. 30 is a large arrow that has been constructed from squares and triangles. To make the arrow, check the positioning in Fig. 31 to see

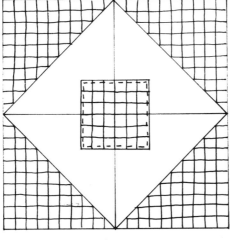

Fig. 28

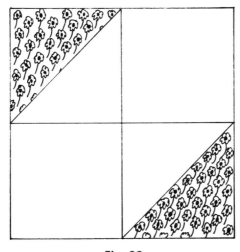

Fig. 29

where the squares and triangles fall. The first row is a dark and light triangle, which makes the first square, sewn to two solid colored squares. The second row has a dark triangle of the first square edge to edge with the dark triangle in row one. This triangle-made square is then sewn to two solid colored squares. The third row is a solid colored square sewn to two triangle-made squares which are placed with the dark triangles edge to edge.

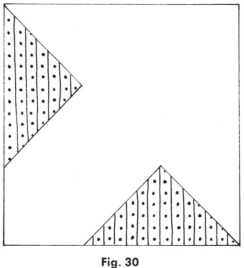

Fig. 30

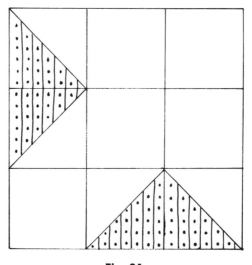

Fig. 31

Cactus Flower

Fig. 32 is a traditional patchwork pattern used for quilts, one that is beautiful and quite simple to do. It's called the Cactus Flower. The unusual feature of this design is that it also requires applique. The crossbar and stem are appliqued after the nine squares are sewn together. To make it, use the

40

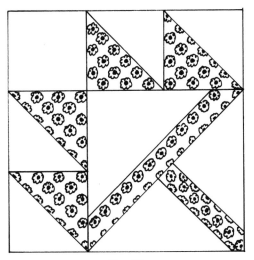

Fig. 32

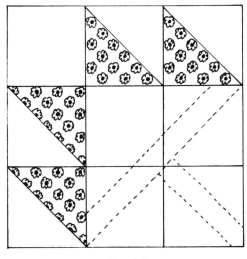

Fig. 33

patterns for the four-inch triangle and four-inch square. Fig. 33 shows how to construct the Cactus Flower.

ROW ONE: One solid colored square is sewn to two triangle-made squares set in a zigzag pattern.

ROW TWO: The triangle-made square, with the printed triangle on its

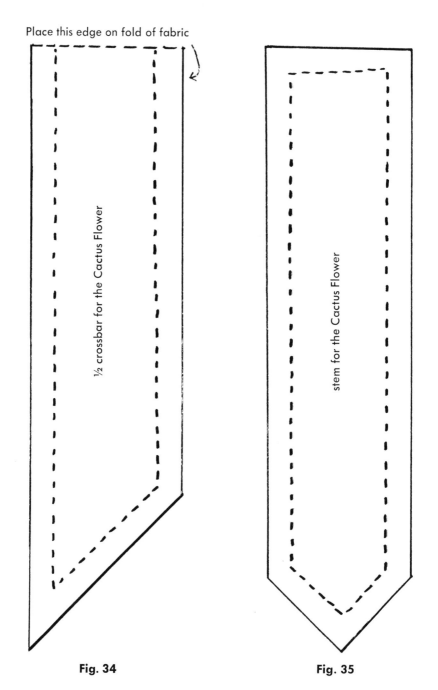

Place this edge on fold of fabric

½ crossbar for the Cactus Flower

stem for the Cactus Flower

Fig. 34   **Fig. 35**

right half, is sewn to two solid colored squares. Sew Row Two to Row One.
ROW THREE: Same as Row Two. Sew Row Three to Row Two.

Cut out the pattern for the Cactus Flower crossbar (Fig. 34). Be sure that you place it on the fold of the fabric. Because this pattern is only half of the crossbar, you must place it on the fold to get the entire piece. Cut the pattern for the stem (Fig. 35) from a printed fabric. Baste down the ¼″ seam allowance for both parts. Pin, then baste the crossbar down. Fit the stem onto the bottom right square on a diagonal. Pin, then baste in place. Sew with a hemming stitch to the squares to complete the Cactus Flower.

Anvil

The Anvil (Fig. 36) looks complicated, but it's only made up of a total of sixteen four-inch squares and four-inch triangles, using two contrasting fabrics, as shown in Fig. 37. This is a traditional pattern that gives a very dramatic effect when many blocks of them are joined together to make a quilt.

ROW ONE: One printed square, two triangle-made squares positioned in a zigzag, one printed square. Set aside.

ROW TWO: The first square is a triangle-made square with the printed triangle on the *left* half. This is sewn to two solid colored squares. The row ends with a triangle-made square with the printed triangle as the outside *right* half. Sew Row Two to Row One.

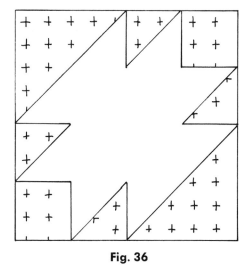

Fig. 36

43

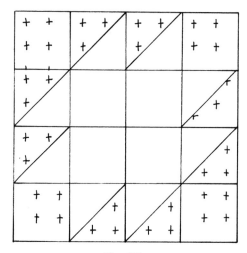

Fig. 37

ROW THREE: Same as Row Two. Sew Row Three to Row Two.

ROW FOUR: One printed square, two triangle-made squares, and one printed square. The *solid* colored triangles of the two middle squares are joined to the *solid* colored squares of Row Three, when Row Four is sewn to Row Three.

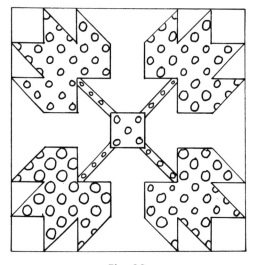

Fig. 38

44

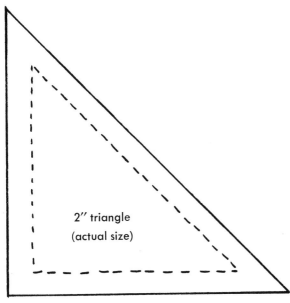

2″ triangle
(actual size)

Fig. 39

Peony

The Peony (Fig. 38) is an exceptionally pretty patchwork pattern. It takes a little more time because there are 49 squares and triangle-made squares to piece together. To make the Peony, use the patterns for the two-inch square (Fig. 17), the two-inch triangle (Fig. 39), and the peony stem (Fig. 40). Like the Cactus Flower, it uses your applique skills, too.

You will need to cut:

20 solid colored squares

13 printed squares

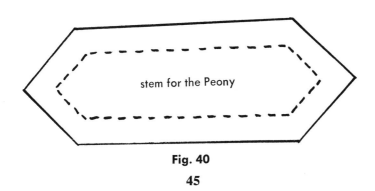

stem for the Peony

Fig. 40

16 solid colored triangles

16 printed triangles

 4 printed stems

Position the triangle-made squares and the squares according to Fig. 41. The four stems are appliqued on the solid colored squares three and five of Rows Three and Five.

Double X

Fig. 42 is a variation of the traditional pattern called the Double X. The Double X is composed of four large squares. The novelty of this pattern is that each of the squares is made up of smaller squares and triangles.

The upper left-hand square and the lower right-hand square are constructed from four two-inch squares. The upper right-hand square and the lower left-hand square are made from two four-inch triangles. You will need to cut the following amounts of squares and triangles to build this Double X:

Four dark colored two-inch squares

Four light colored two-inch squares

Two dark colored four-inch triangles

Two light colored four-inch triangles

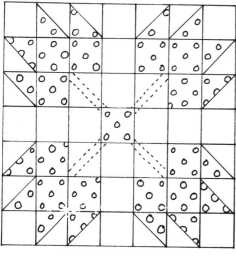

Fig. 41

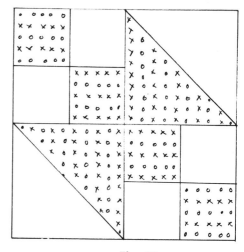

Fig. 42

1. Sew a dark two-inch square to a light two-inch square. Then sew a light two-inch square to a dark two-inch square. Sew the two rows together so that the dark and light squares of each row alternate. This completes the upper left square.

2. Sew a dark four-inch triangle to a light four-inch triangle.

3. Sew the two completed squares together, making sure that the dark and light patterning follows the diagram.

4. To make the next row, follow the same procedure for sewing the two-inch squares and four-inch triangles together.

5. Sew the two rows together.

Grandmother's Fan

Try your hand at Grandmother's Fan—an applique pattern that begs to be made (Fig. 43). It's made up of seven parts, each part in a different patterned fabric.

Cut out all the parts, using the patterns that are provided (Fig. 44). The seam allowances have already been measured.

Sew pieces #1 through #5 together, as shown in Fig. 45. Baste the *outside* edges of #1 and #5, using a ¼" seam allowance. Press.

Baste the seam allowance all around the fan base (#6), as shown in Fig. 46. Press.

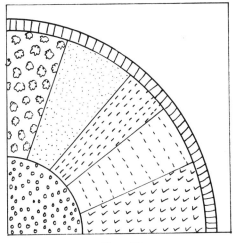

Fig. 43

Fig. 44

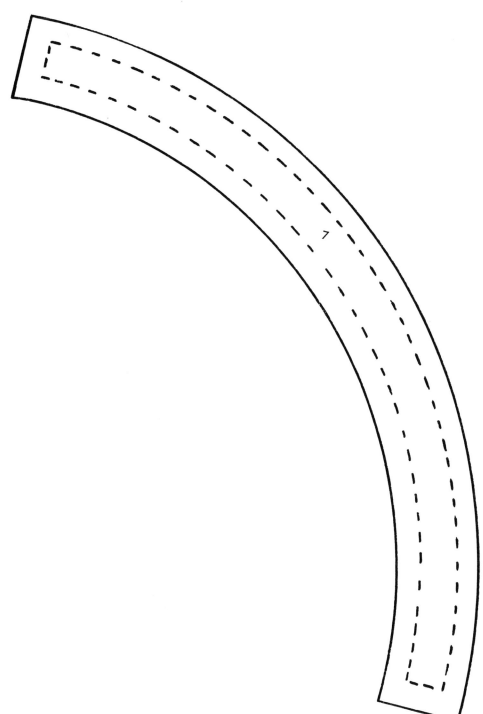

Fig. 44

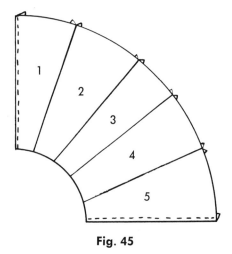

Fig. 45

Fig. 46

Fig. 47

Cut a 6½″ square. This measurement allows for ¼″ seam allowance all around, so that the square will measure 6″ when the hem is turned under. Mark the ¼″ seam allowance with a pencil. Fig. 47 shows how one square should look when measured.

Baste the fan base only to the bottom left-hand corner on the marking for the ¼″ seam allowance, as shown in Fig. 48.

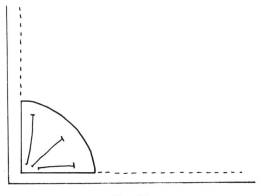

Fig. 48

Slip the five-part fan under the fan base so that the top curve of the fan base covers the ¼" seam allowance on the fan. The outside edge of #1 and the outside edge of #5 should lie flush with the ¼" marked seam allowance on the background square (Fig. 49). Pin, then baste.

Stitch the entire fan in place with small hemming stitches.

Clip the curves of the fan border #7 (See page 52). Baste the seam allowance down, then place the border over the top arc of the fan. The two

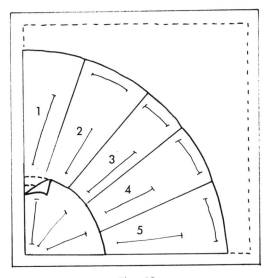

Fig. 49

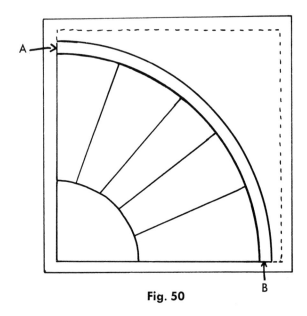

Fig. 50

flat edges of the fan border (A) and (B) should lie on the pencil-marked seam allowance of the background square (Fig. 50). Baste and then sew in place. And, now it's finished.

3

APPLIQUE

Appliques are smaller pieces of fabric sewn to a larger background. They can be made to form an elaborate design, or something quite simple. However, before working on complicated forms, it is a good idea to master the simple shapes.

If you have a large number of pieces of the same shape repeated in your project, it is best to make a template of the shape, remembering to leave a ¼″ for the seam allowance. However, learning how to turn under the seam allowances on three different, but commonly used shapes—the square, triangle, and curve—is important. The patterns are provided, so trace them out, make a template, cut out your fabric and begin.

Square

After cutting your square, fold down the ¼″ seam allowance on the right edge, taking long basting stitches. Since the basting stitches have to be pulled out when the applique is sewn to the background fabric, begin sewing on the *right* side so you can just grasp the knot on the end of the thread and pull the thread out easily. Align the bottom and top edges of the seam allowance as indicated, to keep it even and straight (Fig. 1).

Fold down the top edge seam allowance ¼″, overlapping the right side and keeping the edges even (Fig. 2). Continue folding and basting the seam allowance around the other two sides until the completed square looks like the diagram (Fig. 3) from the inside. End off the basting on the right side. Press with a moderately hot iron.

A nineteenth-century crib quilt in lovely shades of pink, rose, and green in the Spice Pink design. *(Courtesy of America Hurrah.)*

This mid-nineteenth century applique quilt uses twenty-five applique motifs for the central panel. It's called the Album Quilt. *(The Metropolitan Museum of Art, Posthumous Gift of Miss Eliza Polhemus Cobb [Through Mrs. Arthur Bunker], 1952.)*

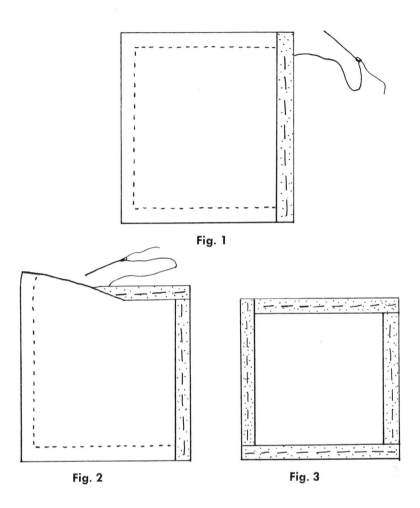

Fig. 1

Fig. 2

Fig. 3

Triangle

The triangle (Fig. 4) is basted like the square, but with a slight variation. Because of its angles, folding the seam allowance makes an overlap of fabric beyond the shape of the triangle. So, to get an even triangle, first baste down the ¼″ seam allowance of the long side of the triangle (Fig. 5).

To solve the problem of overlapping corners, clip the points that extend beyond the side edges, as shown in (A) and (B) in Fig. 6.

Fold the left side ¼″ seam allowance and baste into place (Fig. 7).

Again, clip the point off so that it follows the angle of the long side as shown in (C), Fig. 8.

55

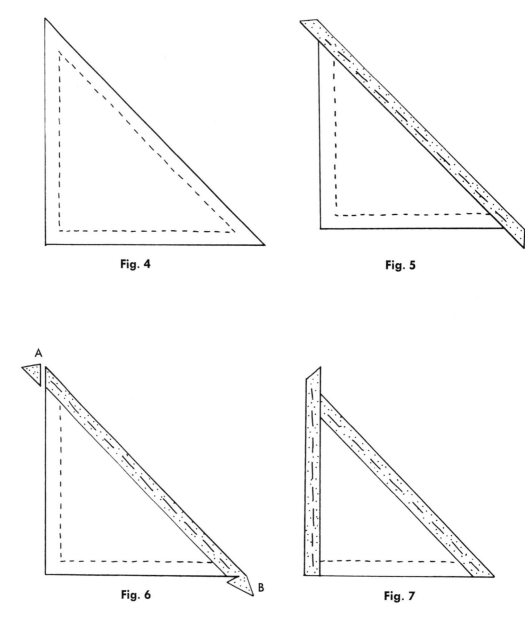

Fig. 4

Fig. 5

Fig. 6

Fig. 7

Fold up the bottom edge to its ¼" seam allowance and baste, as shown in Fig. 9. Clip the final point (D) off for a finished triangle (Fig. 10).

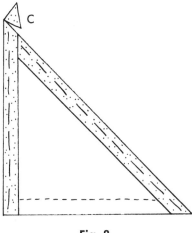

Fig. 8

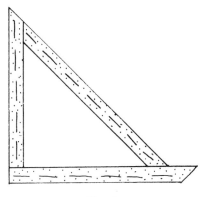

Fig. 9

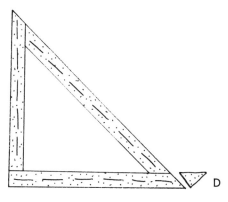

Fig. 10

Curve

Sewing a curved shape is as simple as making a square, but it involves one extra step before you start basting. To turn down the seam allowance around a curve, clipping or notching the edges must be done. Get as close to the seam allowance as you can without actually clipping into it. Clipping curves is a basic sewing rule in dressmaking—it is used for pockets, armholes, sleeves, and necklines.

The curved shape in Fig. 11 shows the ¼″ seam allowance and the spacing for the notches.

57

Left: The central panel of this red, green, and white applique quilt is the American Eagle pattern outlined with leaf stems and flowers. *(Courtesy of The Gazebo.)*

Right: The outer border of the American Eagle quilt picks up the daisy pattern around the eagle to alternate with a lovely bell flower. *(Courtesy of The Gazebo.)*

Begin basting with the knot of the thread on the outside. Fold down the notched pieces on the ¼″ seam allowance *one by one* and baste into place. If the notched pieces overlap when you turn them down, that is all right. Pressing will smooth them out. When you get to a deeper curve (E), it will be better to give it a few extra clips for easier turning (Fig. 12). Continue basting around the curve and when it's completed, it will look like Fig. 13.

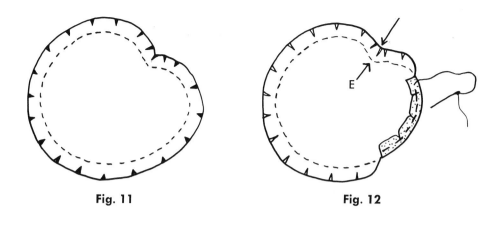

Fig. 11   Fig. 12

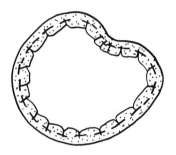

Fig. 13

Centering the Applique on a Square

When making an applique quilt which is made up of squares with appliques on each square (and you'd like each one to be identical), the way to achieve symmetry is by finding the center of each square. One easy way to find the center of a square *without measuring* the width and length with a ruler, is to take the square without the applique (Fig. 14), fold it in half, and crease the material along the width (Fig. 15).

Keep the width folded, then fold it in half again along the length, creasing it where you folded (Fig. 16). The left-hand bottom corner will be the exact center. Push a straight pin into the corner to mark the center and open up the creased square. The pin head should be on the wrong side of the square, with the pin itself coming through the right side (Fig. 17). Mark the center with a lead pencil.

Even if your applique is an odd or asymmetrical shape like an apple-

59

form, you can use this folding technique to get its center too. You can fold it in half, crease, then fold it in half again, then crease, to get the approximate center of it. Push a pin through at its center, then push the pin through the pencil dot center you marked on the square (Fig. 18).

If you're appliqueing a square shape to a larger square, fold the applique in the same folding and creasing technique, marking the center of it with a pin. Push the centered pin through the dot that marks the center of the large square (Fig. 19).

To attach the square applique so that it doesn't get sewn on at an angle,

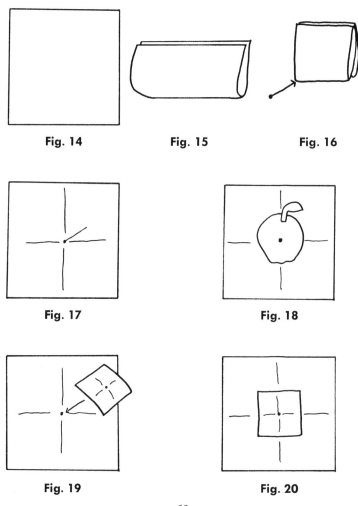

Fig. 14   Fig. 15   Fig. 16

Fig. 17   Fig. 18

Fig. 19   Fig. 20

A beautiful baby quilt with six blocks, each with a different traditional rose pattern. The colors are in pinks and greens on a white background. Made by Fran Ahders for Gabriela Glatzer.

match the creases of the two squares and applique (Fig. 20). Pin down the applique, then baste. Pressing will remove the crease marks.

Here are some simple applique designs that are each about six inches high when finished. You can make multiples of them and set them onto ten-inch squares, to be used for a quilt top. Four of them would make a pillow. Or, perhaps you'll want to use them to decorate jacket backs, purses, or jeans. Since the separate pieces for each applique are small, cotton scraps will work perfectly. Each applique has a pattern which can be traced out and used for cutting each piece. Also included in the directions is an "X-ray" picture of how each separate part fits onto its other parts. The seam allowances have already been marked.

Remember when making an applique:

1. Always measure for the seam allowance. When you cut out these patterns, cut around the *outside* solid line.

2. If you are making more than one of the same design, use the paper pattern to make a template.

3. Cut the pieces carefully.

4. If the shape is curved, clip all the curves before you baste down the seam allowance.

5. Begin basting with the knot on the *right* side of the fabric.

6. Press the basted applique.

7. Before you sew the applique to a patch, or any background fabric, be sure to pin, then baste. Be sure the applique is centered.

8. Sew the applique to the patch or background fabric with a hemming or running stitch. Keep the stitches small and even.

After you have made some practice appliques, you'll be able to make a complicated motif—an original design or one from a pattern.

The Trees

These trees were made from brown and white cotton for the trunks, and a green and white geometrical pattern for the treetops.

Cut out all four parts, using the pattern in Fig. 21.

Baste down the ¼" seam allowances on the tree trunks. Clip the curves on the treetops, then baste down the seam allowances with small stitches. When all four parts are basted, look at the X-ray picture (Fig. 22) to see how the parts will overlap. Sew the parts down like this:

1. Pin, then baste tree trunk #1 to the background fabric. Sew it down with a small hemming stitch.

2. Pin, then baste tree trunk #3 about an inch away from tree trunk #1. Sew it down with a hemming stitch.

3. Pin, then baste treetop #2 to the background fabric, overlapping tree trunk #1 as shown. Sew the treetop in place.

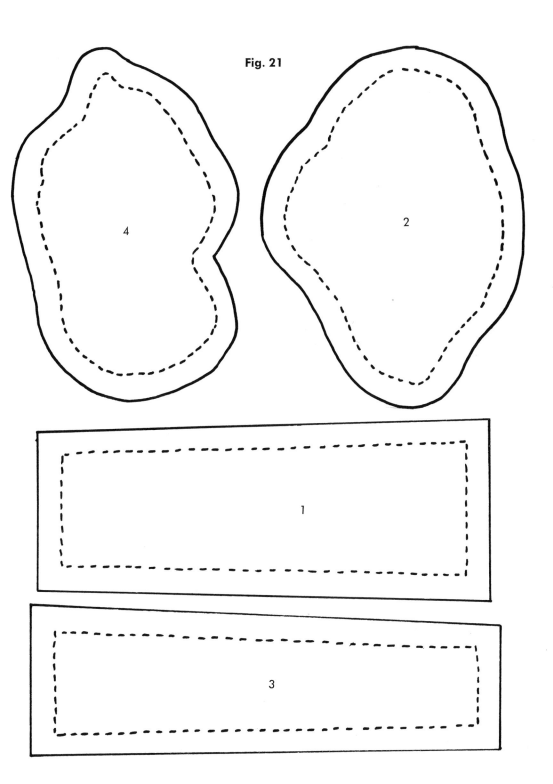

Fig. 21

Fig. 22

The Trees

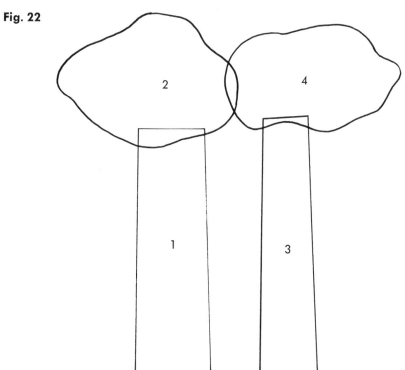

4. Pin, then baste treetop #4, overlapping piece #2 on the edge and the very top of tree trunk #3. Sew in place.

The Rose

This rose was made by using a piece of fabric that was printed with large flowers. You can place the pattern (Fig. 23) on such a flowered print, or use a solid color and achieve that rose-y effect by adding a decorative running stitch after the applique has been sewn down (Fig. 25).

1. Cut out the pieces (Fig. 23).
2. Clip the curves for the stem #1 then baste. down the ¼″ seam allowance. Pin, then baste it to a background fabric and sew it down with a hemming stitch.

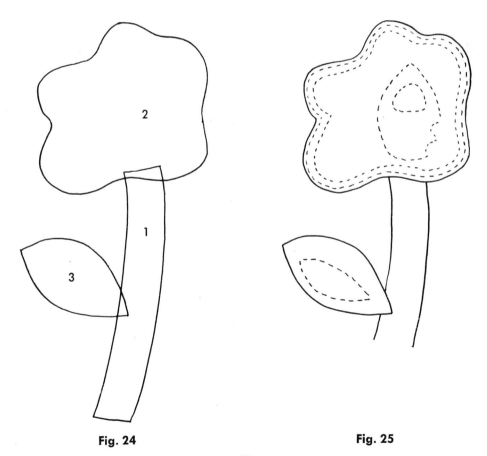

Fig. 24   **Fig. 25**

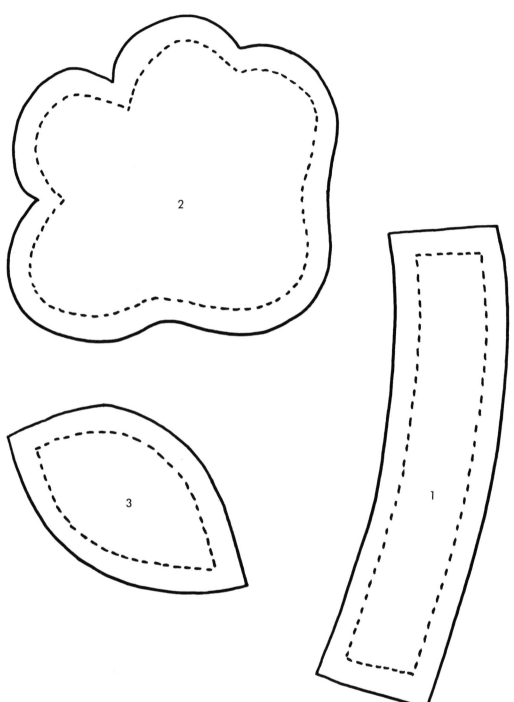

2

3

1

Fig. 23

Fig. 26

3. Baste down the ¼″ seam allowance for the rose, #2, first clipping the curves for a smooth turn. Place it over the stem as shown in the diagram (Fig. 24). Pin, then baste it down. Sew around the rose with a hemming stitch.

4. Clip the curves for the leaf #3 and baste the ¼″ seam allowance. Pin, then baste the leaf to the left side of the stem. Sew it down with a hemming stitch.

5. Using thread of a contrasting color, follow the outside shape of the rose and sew two consecutive rows of small running stitches. Draw a bud shape on the rose with a pencil. Sew over the pencil outline with small running stitches in the contrasting thread. Sew a small leaf shape inside the applique leaf, too (Fig. 25).

Free-Form Felt Flowers

Because felt doesn't unravel when cut, one of the great advantages to using it for appliques is that you won't need to measure or turn under a seam allowance. It's one of the most flexible of fabrics and so easy to use.

Fig. 27

Fig. 28

Fig. 29

Felt Flowers

This applique garden is made from scraps of felt that were just cut out randomly. No patterns were used. The shapes (Fig. 26) are included for you to follow, or you can make your own by turning the felt as you cut, seeing what flowery shapes come out.

When sewing felt shapes to a background fabric, always pin and baste the shapes in place in the order of your design. For this design, cut out all the pieces. Also cut *two* leafless stems—a short one for the first flower and a long one for the fourth flower. Pin, then baste the stems down, as shown in Fig. 27. Pin, then baste the flowers according to Fig. 28, making sure to overlap the flowers slightly on the tops of the stems. Sew to the background fabric with a contrasting thread in an evenly spaced running stitch (Fig. 29).

Double Flower with a Stuffed Bud Center and Stuffed Leaf

Stuffing parts gives your applique a nice, rounded, three-dimensional look. Stuffed appliques are great for bed quilts or for adding special character to any clothing you choose to applique. Another unusual feature to this double flower are tiny yo-yo buds made from a small circle shape.

Double flower with a stuffed bud center and stuffed leaf

yo-yo shape

6

2

4

5

1

3

Fig. 30

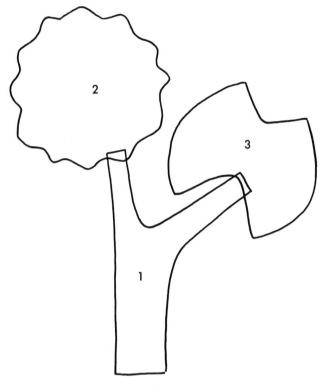

Fig. 31

Note: You can buy polyester fiber fill or kapok for stuffing at any sewing supply or notions shop. They are both washable and do not get lumpy when wet.

1. Cut out all pieces (Fig. 30).

2. Clip the curved joint of the double stem (#1). Baste down the ¼″ seam allowance. Pin and baste to the background fabric, then sew in place with a hemming stitch.

3. Clip the curves of the round flower (#2). Baste down the ¼″ seam allowance. Then, overlapping it on the *left* branch of the stem, as shown in Fig. 31, pin, then baste in place. Attach to the background fabric with a hemming stitch.

4. Clip the curves of the fan-shaped flower (#3), then baste the ¼″ seam allowance. Pin, then baste the flower to the *right* branch of the stem as shown in the X-ray picture. Sew in place with a hemming stitch.

5. To stuff the center bud (#4), clip all around the circular shape of the bud, then baste down the ¼″ seam allowance. Pin, then baste the bud to the center of the round flower, but baste it down *only about three-quarters* of the way around. This will leave the top part of the circular bud open so that it can be stuffed. Sew it down with a running stitch—again, only three-quarters of the way around. Take a small amount of polyester fiber fill or kapok and stuff. Don't overstuff it so that the stitches pull and loosen. Continue sewing the bud closed with a running stitch (Fig. 32).

6. Clip the curves of the leaf and sew down the seam allowance. Pin and baste it a little above halfway up the stem as shown. Sew it down three-quarters of the way around with a small running stitch. Leave the top part of the leaf open as in Fig. 33 and stuff it. Close up the leaf by continuing to sew in a running stitch.

7. To make the yo-yo buds (#6), take a short running stitch close to the edge of the circle. *Do not fold down a seam allowance* for this part. Keep the edges raw (Fig. 34). Pull the thread until the circle gathers tighter and tighter—like pulling closed a drawstring purse—until there's a tiny opening hole in the center (Fig. 35). Flatten the circle so the tiny hole is in the center, hole face up, and all the gathers are distributed equally around it (Fig. 36). Take a backstitch to lock the gathering stitches and retain the yo-yo shape. Make *two* yo-yo buds.

8. Place the yo-yo buds in the top curve of the fan-shaped flower (Fig. 38). Sew them to the background fabric by taking a few small stitches through the tiny center hole, as in Fig. 37.

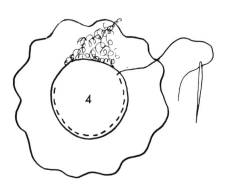

Fig. 32

74

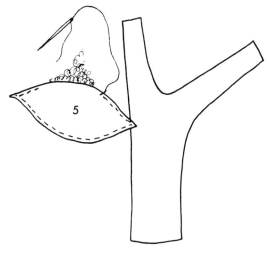

Fig. 33

opening

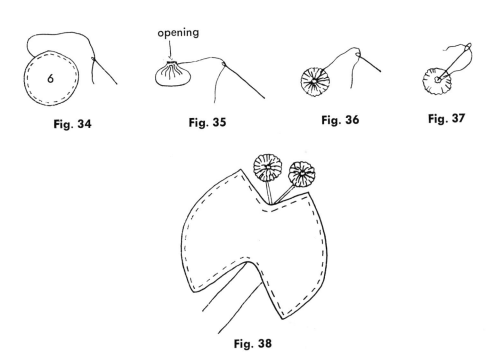

Fig. 34   **Fig. 35**   **Fig. 36**   **Fig. 37**

Fig. 38

9. With green thread, make *two* long stitches to connect each of the buds to the flower (Fig. 38). With white thread, use a running stitch to outline the fan-shaped flower.

SUNBONNET BABY

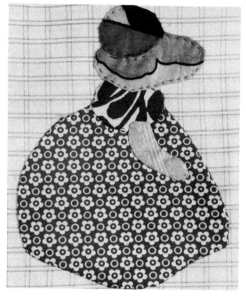

The Sunbonnet Children, also called Sunbonnet Sue and Calico Bill, are one of the variations on the Sunbonnet Baby pattern. Here it's been used as a theme for a crib quilt. (*Courtesy of Appalachian Spring.*)

Sunbonnet Baby

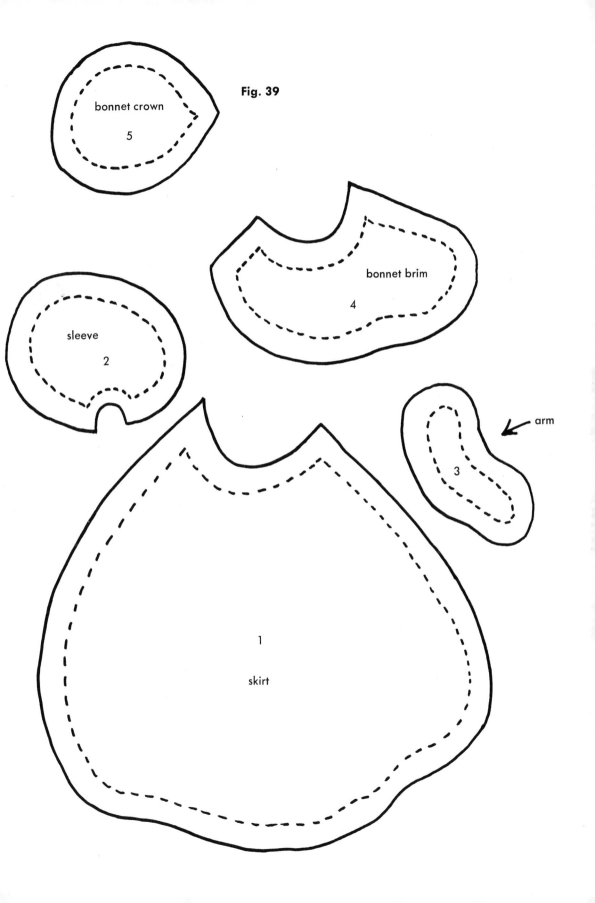

bonnet crown

5

Fig. 39

bonnet brim

4

sleeve

2

arm

3

1

skirt

Sunbonnet Baby

This is a traditional applique especially popular for children's quilts. Each part can be made with a different patterned cotton, or you can mix solid and patterned fabrics.

1. Cut out all the pieces in Fig. 39.

2. Clip the curves around the skirt (#1). Baste down the seam allowance. To center the Sunbonnet Baby on the ten-inch background fabric, first find the center of the ten-inch square by folding and marking the point. The center of the top curve of the skirt should be placed on the center point of the square. The arrow in Fig. 40 shows the center point of the skirt for proper placement. Pin, then baste the skirt to the background. Sew with a hemming stitch.

3. Clip the curves around the sleeve (#2); baste down the seam allowance. Pin, then baste the sleeve to the skirt as shown in Fig. 40, overlapping the skirt top. Sew in place with a hemming stitch.

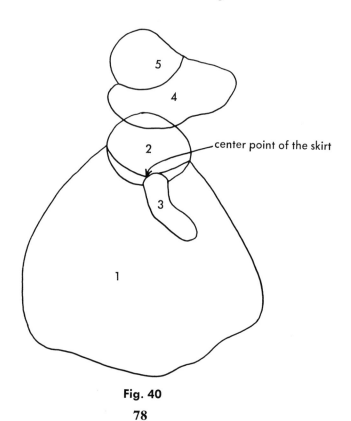

center point of the skirt

Fig. 40

78

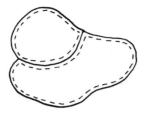

Fig. 41

4. Clip the curves around the arm (#3), and then baste the seam allowance. Pin, then baste the arm onto the skirt, setting the top of the arm into the sleeve's curve. Sew with a hemming stitch.

5. Clip the curves on the bonnet brim (#4); baste the seam allowance. Pin, then baste the bonnet brim so that it overlaps the top of the sleeve as shown in Fig. 40.

6. Clip the curves on the bonnet crown (#5) and baste down the seam allowance. Pin, then baste the bonnet crown so that the base of it fits into the top curve of the brim as shown. Stitch into place with a hemming stitch.

7. Add a decorative stitching with a contrasting color thread by following the curves of the bonnet crown and brim with a short running stitch, as shown in Fig. 41.

FOUR-BLOSSOM FLOWER

Four-Blossom Flower

79

Fig. 42

1
petal

3
right petal

2
center petal

5

8

7

6

4
bottom petal

Four-Blossom Flower

This flower can be made with different patterned cotton fabrics. All the parts will overlap.

1. Cut out all the pieces in Fig. 42.

2. Clip the curves of each piece. Baste down the seam allowances.

3. Pin, then baste the stem (#6) to the background. Sew it in place with a hemming stitch.

4. Pin, then baste the petal base (#5) in place, overlapping the top of the stem about ¼″ (Fig. 43). Leave the *top edge open*, so you can slip in the four petals, as shown in Fig. 44.

5. Take the basted petals and arrange them so that #1 and #3 fit flush with the *outer* edges of *each* side of the petal base (Fig. 45). Pin, but don't baste them into place yet. Slip #2 between them. Pin down #2. Slip in petal #4 so that it overlaps a small section of petals #1, #2, and #3 as

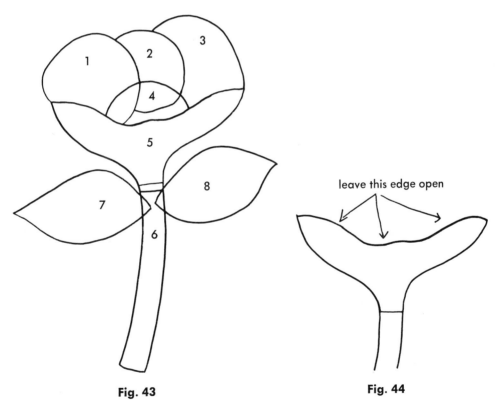

leave this edge open

Fig. 43

Fig. 44

81

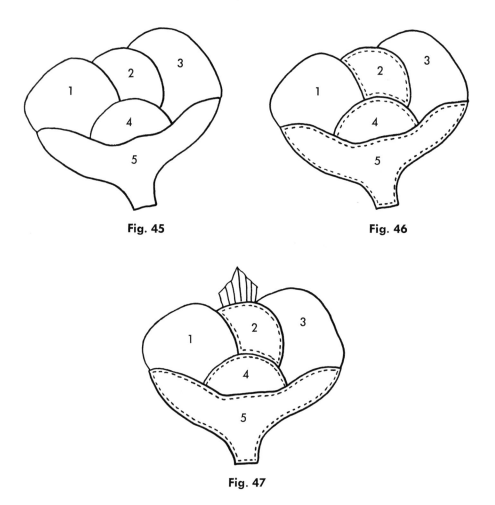

Fig. 45

Fig. 46

Fig. 47

shown. Pin. Baste all the petal parts into place. Baste the top edge of the petal base. Use a hemming stitch to fasten all the petals and the petal base in place.

6. Place the leaves (#7, #8) on either side of the stem as shown in Fig. 43. Pin, baste, then attach with a hemming stitch.

7. Using a constrasting thread, outline the petal base and petals #2 and #4 with a small running stitch as shown in Fig. 46.

8. To add a decorative touch to the flower top, make six graduated lengths of a contrasting thread beginning at the top edge of petal #2 (Fig. 47).

4

QUILTING

Quilting is a simple craft to master, but like any other craft, greater skill is acquired with practice. In making a quilt, or quilting a smaller project like a potholder, there are a few terms to know before beginning.

Parts of the quilt: the *top*, which is the finished patchwork or appliqued blocks; the *center filling*, which is usually cotton batting; and the *back*, or lining, which completes the three layers.

A *block* is a single complete unit of patchwork that has been pieced together to form a particular motif. For example, the Peony or Anvil which is patchworked, would be considered one complete block.

The *quilting stitch* is an evenly spaced, short, *running stitch* which is worked through the three layers that make up the quilt. The running stitch is made in the same way as the one used for seams in patchwork and for sewing appliques in place. Not only does the quilting stitch serve to keep the three layers together, it also adds a decorative flavor.

When beginning the stitch, make a small knot at the end of the thread. Pull the thread from the back layer to the top layer—and tug gently until the knot pulls through the back layer and disappears into the center filling layer. This way the knot will never show. Or, you can start with a back-lock stitch instead of a knot if you prefer.

Materials

You will need a few essentials before you begin:
Sharpened pencils
Ruler

A patchwork quilt that has been quilted with a featherstitch design.

An original morning glory design adds a classic look to this fully quilted cover. (*Courtesy of Heirloom Crafts.*)

Quilting needles. These come in packages at any notions counter. The quilting needle is distinguished from a regular sewing needle by its *shortness*.

Tailor's chalk

Thimble

Cotton batting. Cotton batting is used for the filling between the two layers of fabric. Correct filling is important, since it should be thin enough to work with but not of poor and flimsy quality so it will dissolve or get lumpy when washed. You want your quilt to last! Many companies make a very fine cotton filling which comes in a full quilt size and larger. It is rolled into a cylindrical shape, ready to unroll and use.

Backing. The backing of the quilt, sometimes called the lining, should be made of an easy-to-sew fabric like cotton. Since both sides of the quilt will show when it is finished, the color should coordinate with the front. White cotton is the traditional color used for backing, but let your eye for design decide what will look right.

Quilting hoop (Fig. 1) or adjustable embroidery hoop (Fig. 2). Quilting with a hoop will make stitching easier and more accurate than just holding what will be quilted in your hand. The quilting hoop looks like an embroidery hoop except that the quilting hoop is larger and is attached to a stand. The stand allows for quilting while sitting down, since the stand is at

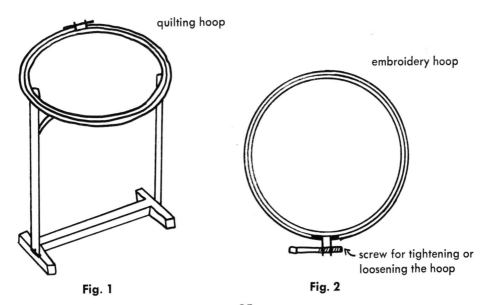

quilting hoop

embroidery hoop

screw for tightening or loosening the hoop

Fig. 1   **Fig. 2**

table height. Smaller quilting hoops are available which can be placed on a table. These small hoops resemble a mirror on a stand.

Quilting Frame. The quilting frame is used when doing an all-over quilting design on a full-sized quilt. The quilting frame resembles the rectangular frame of a table *without* the solid wood top. Movable bars on the two long sides of the frame allow the quilt to be turned and rolled over one bar to the other as it is worked on. It's a rolling motion much like pulling down a window shade when one bar, on the top, takes up the length of the fabric from the bar on the bottom. So, as the quilt is stitched, the stitched part can be rolled onto one bar, fastened into place, and another part of the quilt can then be stitched. Although it is easier to work on a quilting frame for an entire quilt, the quilting can be done with the smaller quilting hoop, moving it to a new position as necessary.

Preparing the Layers

Spread the backing down on a clean, flat surface. Place the cotton batting, measured to size, onto the backing. Baste it down to the backing as shown in Fig. 3. Be sure that both the backing and cotton batting are free of bumps. Both layers should be perfectly smooth before basting. Begin basting from the center and work out toward the edges and sides.

Spread the top of the quilt down, making sure that it's smooth and well pressed. Baste it to the other two layers, working from the center, out toward the edges. Also baste along the four sides, as shown in Fig. 4.

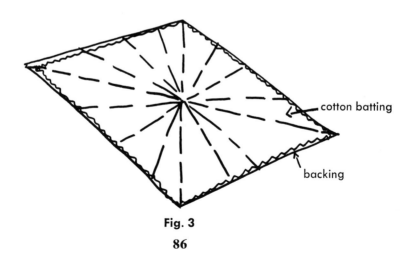

cotton batting

backing

Fig. 3

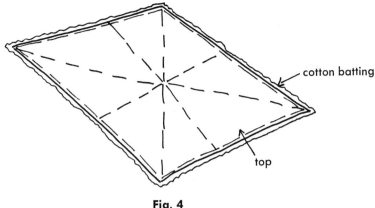

Fig. 4

Quilting Patterns

You can quilt through the three layers without using a template of a quilting pattern. This is done by *tracing the outline* of the square blocks, as in Fig. 5, with short quilting stitches, or tracing around both the applique shape and the block, as in Fig. 6.

If you are going to repeat a quilting design throughout the quilt, you should make a template. Decide on the pattern and cut out your cardboard template. The quilting pattern is always traced onto the top of the quilt *after* the three layers have been basted together. Place the template on what will be quilted and trace around it with a pencil or tailor's chalk. Tailor's chalk comes in pencil form, in white or pale blue. These colors are perfect for tracing a pattern onto a dark or light fabric. The quilting stitches should be

Fig. 5

Fig. 6

Below: A simple stuffed toy is made more interesting with an appliqued flower on its side and quilted flowers on its ears. (*Courtesy of Appalachian Fireside Crafts Organized by Save the Children Federation. Photograph by Jan W. Faul.*)

Above: A Lone Star patchwork pattern has been quilted on the background fabric with a corresponding star pattern. (*Courtesy of Appalachian Spring.*)

Fig. 7

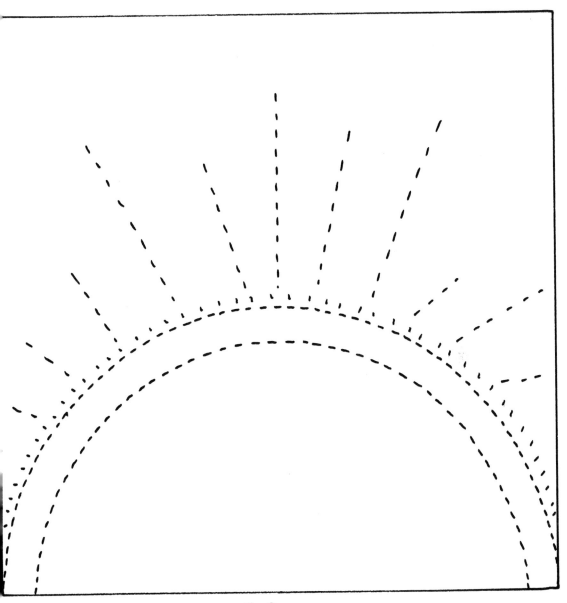

Fig. 8

made over the pencil markings—finely spaced, short, running stitches.

Practice with straight lines in all combinations—crossed lines, triangles, and squares. Once you have the knack of stitching through the three layers, try your hand at curves or intricately detailed shapes.

Here are some patterns which you can trace out and use:

Fig. 7—An all-over Diamond.

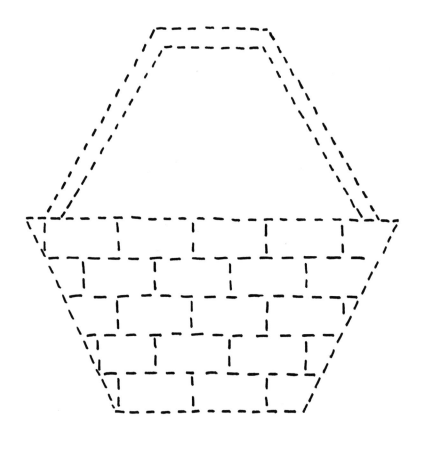

Fig. 9

Fig. 8—A simple Sunburst, which works well for solid color blocks. You can make two templates—one for the outside curve and one for the inside curve. The radiating lines can be made by placing a ruler down on the top layer and making small dashes.

Fig. 9—A Flower Basket, which has been adapted from a patchwork pattern. Make a template for the outline of the basket and then, using a ruler, draw in the dashes for the woven pattern.

Fig. 10

Fig. 10—The Clam Shell, which is just a half circle that is repeated by tracing the shape from the bottom upwards.

Fig. 11—The Strawberry, an excellent border pattern that can also be used for appliques.

Fig. 12—The Butterfly. Trace the outline and duplicate the inside curves as shown.

Fig. 13—A Traditional Flower that has the center bud made by crossing

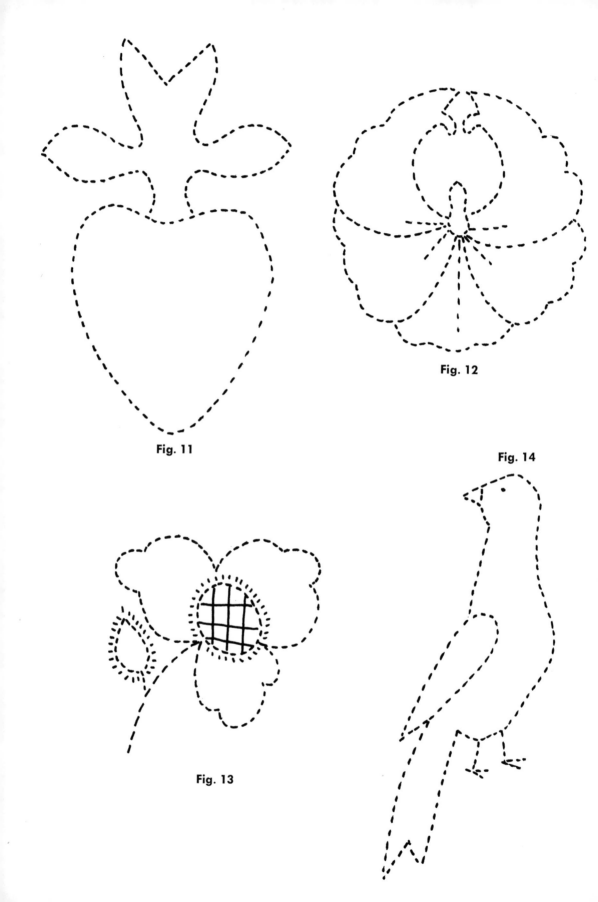

Fig. 11

Fig. 12

Fig. 13

Fig. 14

Fig. 15

Fig. 16

Fig. 17

long stitches. Trace the outline of the flower, then fill in the center bud stitches and radiating stitches.

Fig. 14—A Whimsical Bird. Trace the outline.

Figs. 15, 16, 17—Decorative leaf shapes. Trace the outline and fill in the veins with short stitches, according to the drawing, or improvise your own decorative design.

Using an Adjustable Quilting Hoop or Embroidery Hoop

Now that the layers have been basted together and the quilting pattern marked on the top layer, you are ready to place it in the hoop for sewing.

Open the two parts of the embroidery hoop. Place the piece to be quilted on the smaller hoop. Press the outer ring down over the inside ring and piece to be quilted. Be certain that it's smooth and that there are no wrinkles. Tautness is important.

Hold the hoop so that it rests between the thumb and index finger. Your index finger should push *upwards from underneath* the hoop so that the backing is sure to catch the needle and thread as it comes down from the top. With your left thumb, press down on the top of the fabric and with your index finger, push up at the same time as you sew. This will keep the three layers together so that the needle and thread go completely through (Fig. 18).

Hold the needle higher than usual between the thumb and index finger, so that it seems like you are going into the material on more of a vertical plane, as in Fig. 19.

Fig. 18

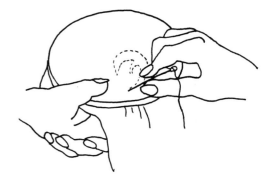

Fig. 19

Go in through all layers, catching the back too, and come back up to the top, taking a short stitch. Eventually you will be able to make a few quilting stitches at a time, as if you were just basting a seam. Practice!

When you are quilting on a quilting hoop, the technique varies slightly. Since the quilting hoop is on a stand, you needn't hold the hoop. What you must remember to do, though, as you stitch, is to *push upwards* from underneath with your index finger and *press down* with your thumb.

Binding

When you have finished all the quilting, trim away the excess batting and lining, using the top of the quilt as your cutting guide (Fig. 20). Now it's ready for binding the edges.

Measure the quilt and cut four strips of contrasting fabric that will each be sewn to one side. Bindings can be any size you choose, although the traditional width is about two inches. This means that if you want a two-inch binding, you will need a four-inch wide strip, since the binding gets folded in half. In addition, don't forget to add on a seam allowance that includes the amount needed for sewing the binding to the front *and* to the back. Figuring two ½" seam allowances, to get the desired two-inch completed binding, the exact width of the fabric will be *five* inches—½" seam allowance for the front, four inches for the folded binding, and a ½" seam allowance to turn under on the back.

An easy way to attach the binding is to sew it on strip by strip. The top and bottom of the quilt should be the same width (A in Fig. 21) and the

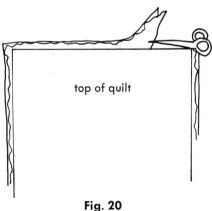

top of quilt

Fig. 20

95

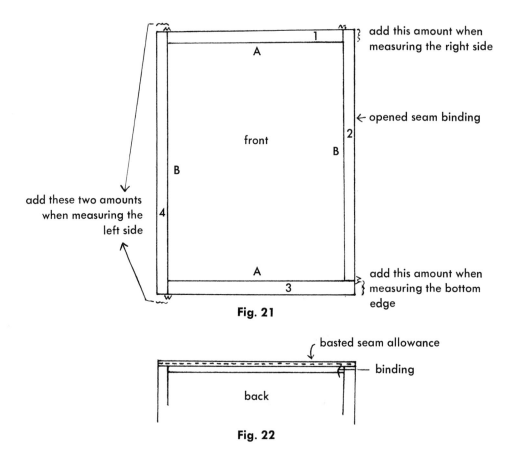

add this amount when measuring the right side

← opened seam binding

A

front

B

B

add these two amounts when measuring the left side

A

add this amount when measuring the bottom edge

Fig. 21

basted seam allowance

binding

back

Fig. 22

sides should be the same length (B in Fig. 21).

Begin by measuring a strip that is the exact width of the top edge. Sew it down, right side to right side, with a short running stitch, or sew it on by machine.

To measure the right-hand side, include the dimensions of the top binding in measuring. Begin at the tip of the already sewn-on binding down to the bottom edge of the quilt (Fig. 21).

To measure the bottom edge binding, include the dimensions from the right side (Fig. 21).

Measure the left-hand strip by including the widths from *both* the top and bottom strips (Fig. 21).

When the four strips are sewn on, baste down the seam allowance on the outside edges of all four sides (Fig. 22). Fold the binding in half and

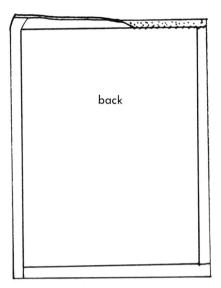

Fig. 23

turn to the back. Sew the binding down with a hemming stitch (Fig. 23).
Sew the corners together with a slip stitch or a very small-spaced hemming
stitch.

5

EMBROIDERY STITCHES

Embroidery Stitches

Embroidery stitches add a decorative touch to appliqued squares, triangles, or odd-shaped pieces such as those used in crazy quilting. These stitches are easy to master if you follow these rules. Use embroidery floss in an appropriate color.

1. Each stitch is made like a long running stitch—go in and out of the fabric in one motion. *Don't* go into the fabric and pull the needle and thread

A detail of the rose quilt showing one block that has been personalized with an embroidered dedication. Made by Fran Ahders for Gabriela Glatzer.

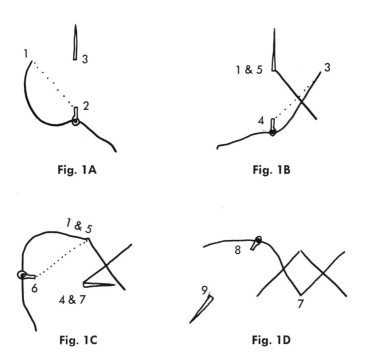

Fig. 1A

Fig. 1B

Fig. 1C

Fig. 1D

through from the back and *then* come out to the front again. Hold the needle at an angle so you can go in and out in one motion.

2. Keep the stitches the same size to get a nice even look.

3. Practice.

The Horizontal Cross-Stitch

A. Knot the thread and bring the needle out from the back to the front. The starting stitch is the *only* one that is not done in one step. Place the needle on a diagonal and go in to point 2 and with the same movement come out at point 3 (Fig. 1A).

B. Bring the thread out at point 3. To make the cross, go in at point 4 and, with one motion, come out in the same hole as point 1. Point 1 and point 5 are the same (Fig. 1B).

C. To start another cross-stitch, with the thread at point 5, cross horizontally to the left and go in at point 6 and out at point 7. Point 7 is the same as point 4. Pull thread through (Fig. 1C).

D. To complete the second cross-stitch, bring thread from point 7 going

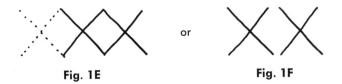

Fig. 1E   or   **Fig. 1F**

in at point 8 and out at point 9 in one motion (Fig. 1D).

    E. Your completed cross-stitches will look like Fig. 1E.

    F. If you like, you can space the cross-stitches, keeping them the same size but not using one point to join two stitches (Fig. 1F).

The Vertical Cross-Stitch

    The vertical cross-stitch is made in the same way as the horizontal cross-stitch, except that the needle goes downwards instead of to the side.

    1. Knot the thread and bring it out from the back to the front. Cross on the diagonal, going to the left, and insert the needle at point 2. Bring the needle out in one motion to point 3. Pull thread through (Fig. 2A).

    2. To complete the first cross-stitch, bring the needle from point 3 over

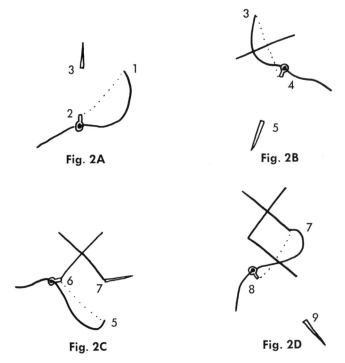

Fig. 2A   **Fig. 2B**

Fig. 2C   **Fig. 2D**

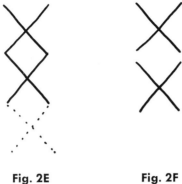

Fig. 2E   Fig. 2F

to point 4 and out at point 5. Pull thread through and the cross is completed (Fig. 2B).

3. To begin the second cross-stitch vertically, bring the needle from point 5 up to point 6 and, in one motion, come out at point 7. Point 6 goes into the same hole as point 2. Point 7 goes into the same hole as point 4 (Fig. 2C).

4. To complete the second cross-stitch, bring the needle out at point 7 and cross down, going into point 8 and, in one motion, come out at point 9. Pull thread through and the second cross-stitch is done (Fig. 2D).

5. Fig 2E shows vertical row of cross-stitches, going into the same point holes. Fig. 2F shows the vertical cross-stitch spaced.

The Blanket Stitch

The blanket stitch (or buttonhole stitch) is perfect for decorating edges of appliques. To make the blanket stitch, it's important to remember this: Always keep the thread *under* the needle so the loop can be formed.

1. Knot the thread and bring the needle out on the background fabric so that it's right *at the edge* of your applique, as at point 1 in Fig. 3A. Hold the thread loop down with your thumb while you bring the needle up about ¼ ″ and into the applique at point 2 in Fig. 3B. Go through both the applique and the background fabric and, in one motion, bring the needle out of the background fabric—*at the edge* of the applique, which is point 3 as shown in Fig. 3B—and with the thread *under* the needle. Pull the thread through to finish the first stitch.

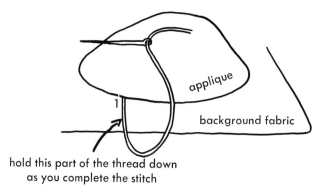

applique

background fabric

hold this part of the thread down
as you complete the stitch

Fig. 3A

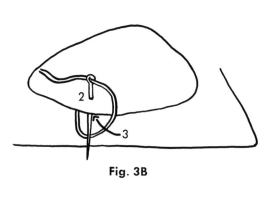

2

3

Fig. 3B

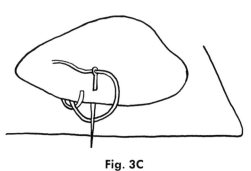

Fig. 3C

2. To begin a second blanket stitch, bring the needle up about ¼", go through both the applique and background fabric, and come out at the edge of the applique as in Fig. 3C. Don't forget to always hold the loop of the thread down so that the thread is always under the needle.

This was a very simply made, patchwork-bordered, appliqued quilt. The two basic shapes were the square—either set down at right angles or tipped to the side—and the yo-yo. Each square has been imaginatively embroidered with decorative stitches.

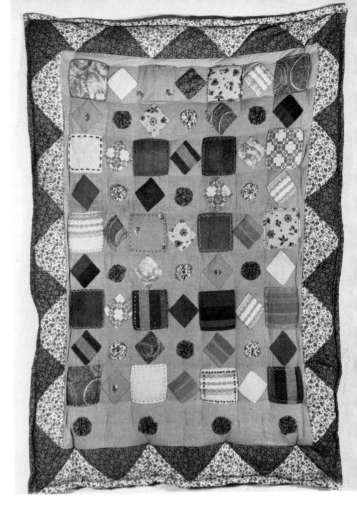

Detail of embroidery

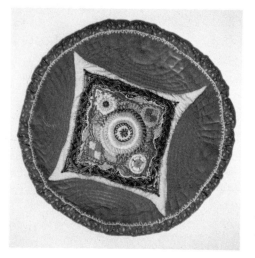

Left: Embroidery stitches accent the shape and add texture and dimension to this flat quilted pillow. Made by Virginia Davis.

Below: An elaborately done, eighteenth-century German patchwork cover highlighted with embroidery details. (*The Metropolitan Museum of Art, Bequest of Helen Hay Whitney, 1945.*)

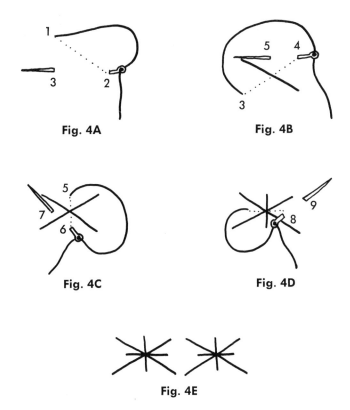

Fig. 4A

Fig. 4B

Fig. 4C

Fig. 4D

Fig. 4E

The Star

This is a variation of the cross-stitch with an additional two short stitches that make another cross through the center.

1. Knot your thread and bring the needle out from the back at point 1 as in Fig. 4A. Bring the needle down to the right and in at point 2. In one motion, come out at point 3.

2. From point 3, cross up to point 4 (Fig. 4B). Bring the needle out at point 5. Point 5 should be the mid-point between points 1 and 4.

3. To make the first half of the small cross, bring the needle from point 5 down straight into point 6 (Fig. 4C). In one motion, come out at point 7. Point 7 should lie between point 1 and point 3.

4. To finish the star, go from point 7 into point 8 and out in one motion to point 9 (Fig. 4D). Point 8 should lie between point 4 and point 2. Point 9 will begin another star stitch.

5. Fig. 4E shows two spaced star stitches.

6

THINGS TO MAKE

Here are projects for you to make, using your knowledge of patchwork, applique, and quilting. All the projects are simple and fun to do. You can also experiment and improvise other designs if you like.

Appliqued Bib and Shorts

A simple pair of summer shorts are made just a bit more personalized by adding your own applique iris to the bib front. Shorts patterns in this style

Left: Appliqued bib and shorts.   **Right: Detail of iris applique.**

are readily available from most sewing pattern companies. The iris applique, which is a traditional applique pattern used for blocks in making bed quilts, can be made from any fabric. Since felt doesn't need to be hemmed, it is easy to make the iris from this fabric for the detachable bib. To use this iris pattern when not using felt, measure ¼" around each part of the iris for the seam allowance and make an applique in the usual way.

Materials:
The required amount of denim for shorts and bib
9" × 8" pieces of red, lavender, and kelly green felt. Get *one* rectangle in each color.
Small amount of 100 per cent polyester fiber fill to stuff the applique
Needle and white thread
Pins
Scissors

Follow the instructions for making the shorts. Cut out the bib, but do not complete it until the applique has been done.

Make a tracing of the iris parts (Fig. 1). Using a paper pattern, cut one petal #1 and one petal #2 in lavender. Cut one petal #1 and one petal #2 in red. You will have four petals in all—two in lavender and two in red. Make a paper pattern of the stem #3, and cut one out of kelly green felt. Make a paper pattern of the leaves and cut two of leaf #4 and one of leaf #5 in kelly green felt.

Using only the *front* piece of the bib—the other half is the facing—mark the seam allowance all around the front. Do *not* sew your applique to an already faced bib.

Find the center point on the bottom edge of the bib front by folding only once, lengthwise. Pin, then baste the stem on the bottom edge, as shown in Fig. 2. Place the leaves, #4 and #5, just slightly *under* the edge of the stem. There should be two leaves on the right side and one leaf on the left side. Pin, then baste the leaves to the bib front.

Thread a needle with white thread and sew the stem to the bib front with short running stitches. Begin sewing the stem on the *left side* edge and continue up and around, leaving the bottom edge open so you can stuff the

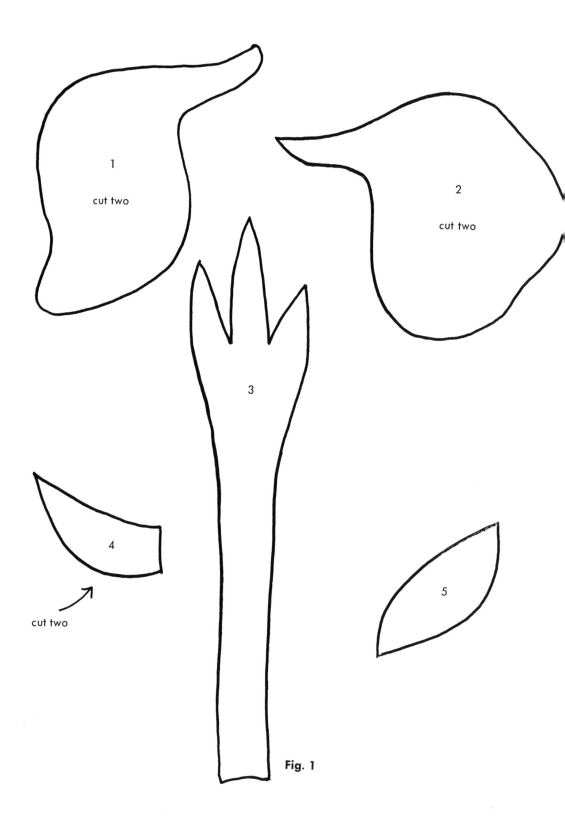

1
cut two

2
cut two

3

4

cut two

5

Fig. 1

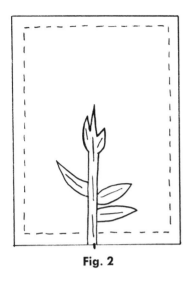

Fig. 2

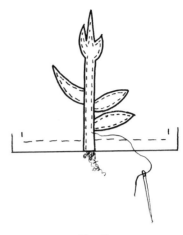

Fig. 3

entire stem. Sew the leaves down with white thread, taking short stitches.

Take a tiny amount of polyester fiber fill and stuff the stem (Fig. 3). Use a pencil to push the polyester high into the three-part point of the stem, and sew the bottom closed. Don't overstuff because the felt will get lumpy and pull too tightly against the stitches.

Place one red petal #1 and one red petal #2 on either side of the long center point of the stem as shown in Fig. 4. Pin, then baste down. Thread a needle with white thread and sew the petals to the bib front, leaving about an inch of the top open to stuff (Fig. 4). Using tiny amounts of polyester fiber fill, stuff each petal and sew it closed.

Position the top two petals, lavender petals #1 and #2. This time, put petal #2 (the larger one) on the left side and #1 (the smaller one) on the right side. Pin the petals and baste. Using white thread, sew around both petals, leaving one inch open to stuff. Stuff the petals. Sew them closed (Fig. 5).

Now sew the bib front to the bib facing. With the *right* sides together, sew around three sides and about an inch or so on either side on the bottom. Clip the corners and turn the right side out (Fig. 6). Follow the directions on the pattern direction sheet for making the straps and for sewing the bottom of the bib.

If you want to attach the straps to the bib with snaps instead of button-

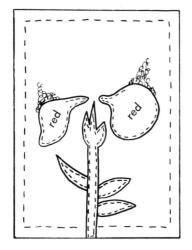

Fig. 4

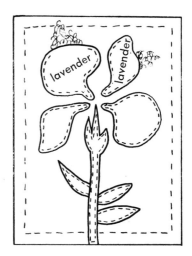

Fig. 5

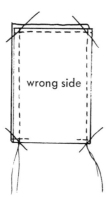

wrong side

Fig. 6

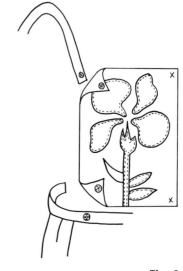

Fig. 8

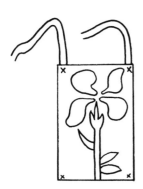

Fig. 7

holes, sew snaps where the "Xs" are marked on the diagram (Fig. 7). Sew the snaps to the inside facing of the bib and to the outside of the straps, as shown in Fig. 8, for the top. Sew snaps to the outside of the waistband and to the bottom corners of the bib facing for the bottom of the bib front (Fig. 8).

Fried Egg Potholder

Add a touch of whimsy to your kitchen with a quilted fried egg-shaped potholder. The potholder is made in four parts—two egg yolks and two whites. The egg is quilted in brown or yellow thread. If made of felt it need not be bound around the edges and you won't need seam allowances.

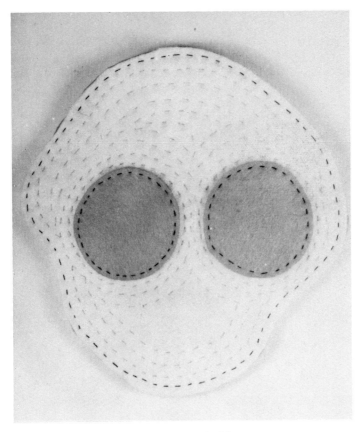

Fried Egg Potholder

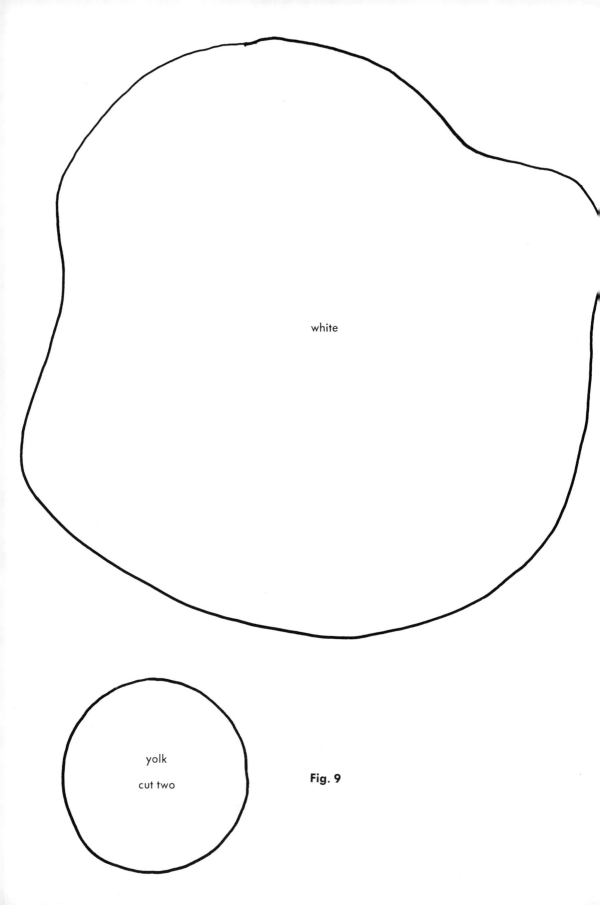

white

yolk

cut two

Fig. 9

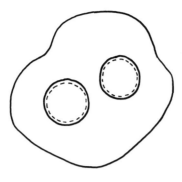

Fig. 10

Materials:
Two 9″ × 8″ pieces of white felt
One 9″ × 8″ piece of yellow felt
Yellow thread
Brown thread
Cotton batting
Pins
Scissors

Trace out the pattern for the fried egg and make a paper pattern (Fig. 9).
Cut *only one egg white* and two egg yolks. The second white felt 9″ rectangle
will be used for the backing.

Place the egg yolks toward the center of the egg white you have cut out
and pin. Baste. Sew them down with a small running stitch in brown thread
(Fig. 10).

To begin quilting the fried egg: Cut a piece of cotton batting and place

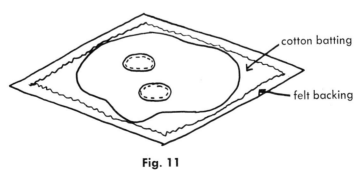

cotton batting

felt backing

Fig. 11

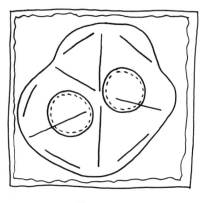

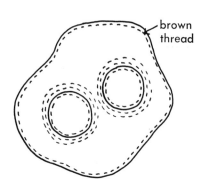
brown thread

Fig. 12   Fig. 13

it on the 9" rectangle of white felt. Baste together. Now position the appliqued egg white on top of the batting (Fig. 11). Baste the three parts together, taking long stitches from the center of the egg, and extending the stitches out toward the edges (Fig. 12).

Thread a needle with brown thread and quilt through the three layers, working close to the outside edge. Make one row of brown quilting stitches to follow the outside curve of the egg (Fig. 13).

With yellow thread, quilt two concentric circles around each egg yolk as in Fig. 13.

Following the shape of the egg white, work three more rows around the top of the egg in yellow thread and four rows along the bottom, as in Fig. 16.

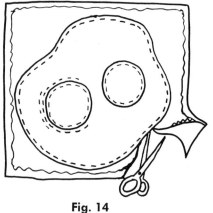

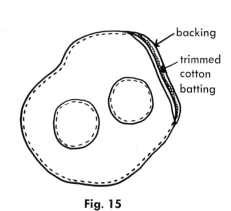
backing

trimmed cotton batting

Fig. 14   Fig. 15

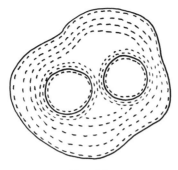

Fig. 16

Trim off the excess batting and felt backing by following the lines of the top appliqued egg white, as in Fig. 14.

Trim the batting between the two egg white layers to neaten the egg, as in Fig. 15.

WALL HANGING

Wall Hanging

Wall Hanging

Making this simple wall hanging is almost like painting a picture. Trees, a running girl, birds, and flowers are all made of felt and sewn to a green and yellow background. A short running stitch keeps each piece in place.

Materials:

¼ yard of green felt, 72″ wide

½ yard of yellow felt, 72″ wide

9″ × 8″ pieces of felt in the following colors: one each— violet, red, orange, chartreuse, white

Fig. 17

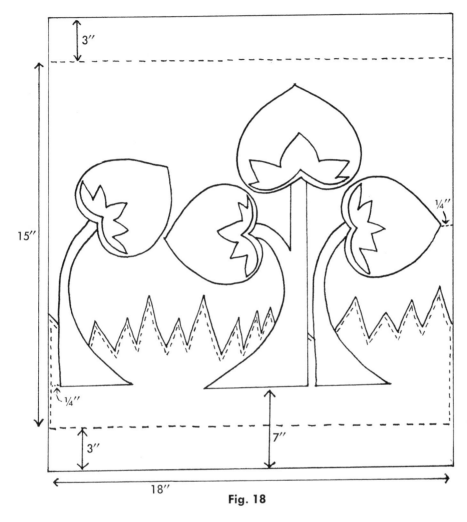

Fig. 18

Two 9″ × 8″ pieces of brown felt

1½ yards of red yarn

Two 18″ curtain rods that are ⅜″ in diameter. (Or, you can get a 36″ long dowel rod in any hardware store or lumberyard. Cut it in two 18″ parts.)

Thread

Fig. 17 shows how all the parts are positioned and where to stitch them. The dotted lines across the top and bottom indicate where to sew to make a casing for the rods.

117

Fig. 18 shows the measurements for placing the trees. All other parts are overlapped on the trees or will be placed around them.

Trace out all the pattern pieces (Fig. 19), make a paper pattern for each, and cut the felt as follows:

Three small tree tops in dark green

Three small tree leaves in chartreuse

Two flowers in violet

Two flower stems and leaves in chartreuse

One large tree trunk in brown

Two small tree trunks in brown

Girl's head in white

Girl's arms in white

Girl's legs in red

Girl's dress in orange

Girl's hair in brown

Two birds in red

One bird in orange

Two butterflies in violet

Two small free-form flowers for the girl's hair, one in yellow and one in red.

Now cut a piece of yellow felt 17½" wide by 15" long, and a piece of green felt 17½" wide by 8½" long. Zigzag cut the green felt on the top edge to get a grassy effect. Improvise the lengths and widths of each piece of grass. Attach the zigzag section to the bottom of the yellow section. Measure to get each side even. Be sure that the green and yellow parts, when sewn together, add up to 21" as shown in Fig. 20.

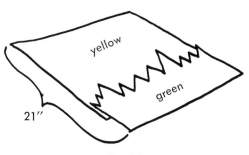

yellow

green

21"

Fig. 20

Fig. 19

orange

red

red

cut two

Fig. 19

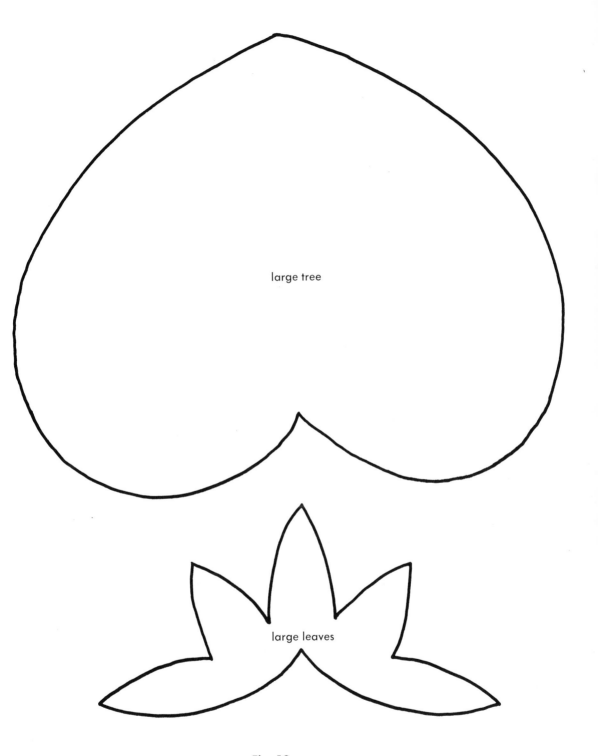

large tree

large leaves

Fig. 19

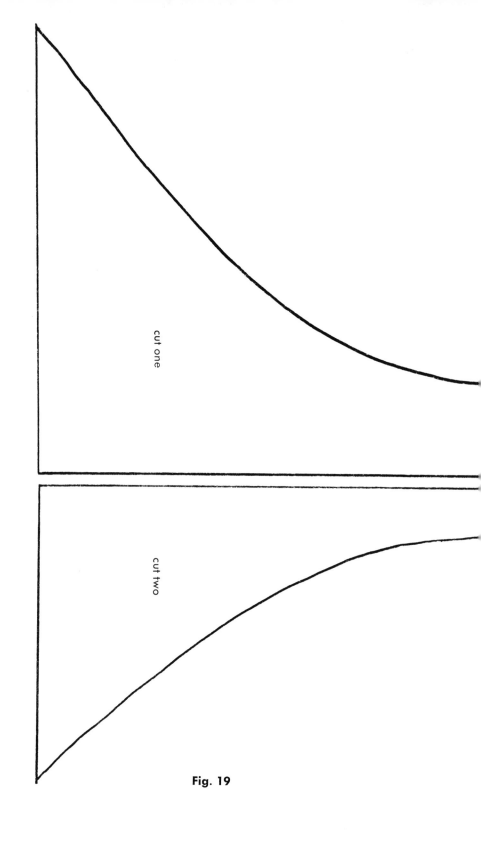

cut one

cut two

Fig. 19

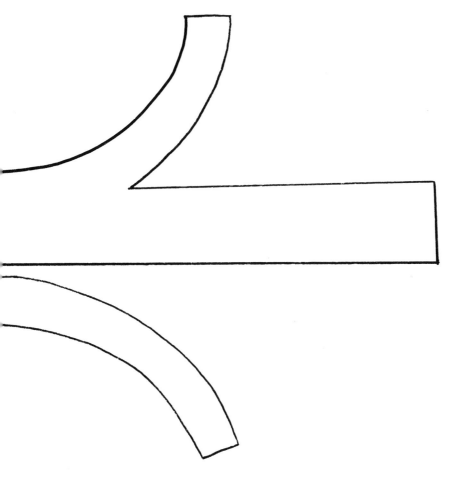

Fig. 19

flower

cut two

small tree

cut three

small leaves

cut three

Fig. 19

Pin, then baste the grass to the yellow sky. Stitch the grass to the sky with white thread, taking small running stitches.

Assembling the parts:

Pin, then baste the tree trunks so that their bases are 7″ from the bottom edge of the grass. (See Fig. 18.) The large double tree trunk is spaced ¼″ from the tree trunk to its right. The small tree trunk is positioned ¼″ from the *left* side edge. Fig. 18 shows the three tree trunks in position. Sew them in place with a small running stitch in white thread.

Attach the treetops, as shown in Fig. 21. They should overlap the ends of the branches, but should not touch each other. The large treetop goes on the end of the straight trunk of the large tree. The three smaller treetops go on the curved branches. Stitch down with white thread, after pinning and basting.

Pin, then baste the tree leaves to the treetops. Sew in place with dark green thread.

To make the girl, first place her face and hair so that they lie over the

Fig. 21

125

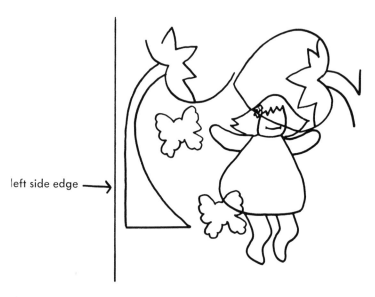

left side edge →

Fig. 22

second treetop from the left. (See Fig. 22.) Pin, then baste. Pin and baste her dress. Pin and baste her arms so that the edges of her arms are set evenly against the sides of her dress. Pin, then baste her legs so that the edges of them fit on the curve of the hem of her dress. Her hair is sewn with white thread, her face in white thread, and the dress in brown thread. After her dress is sewn down, make two more rows of stitching under the neckline. Sew a pocket design with brown thread. Her arms are sewn with white thread. The legs are sewn with white thread. Using red thread, make a smile, using a backstitch. Tack the two free-form flowers onto the left side of her hair with two backstitches each.

Pin, then baste the butterflies on. One butterfly has one wing that overlaps the left bottom edge of the girl's skirt. The second butterfly goes on at an angle, directly under the tree leaves of the left tree (Fig. 22). Use white thread to sew.

Pin, then baste the flowers and flower stems to the grass on the right side of the hanging. The first flower should overlap the pointed edge on the base of the tree trunk, as shown in Fig. 23. The second flower overlaps the first flower just a fraction of an inch. Sew with pink thread.

FINISHING: To make a casing for the rod or dowel, measure 3″ down

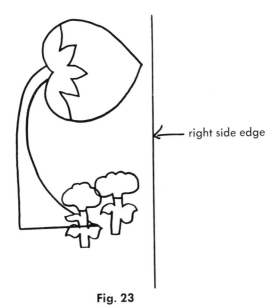

right side edge

Fig. 23

from the top edge and 3″ up from the bottom edge. Mark across the top and bottom edges with pencil or a piece of white tailor's chalk. This is the line you will be sewing on (Fig. 25).

Measure 1½″ from the top and bottom edges, and fold them down (Fig. 26). Pin along the edge (Fig. 27).

Fig. 24

127

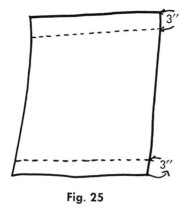

Fig. 25

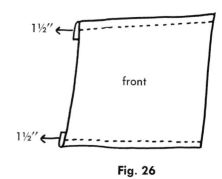

front

Fig. 26

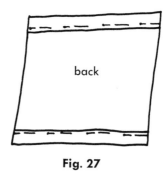

back

Fig. 27

With white thread, make a short running stitch across the top and bottom marked lines. Insert the two dowels in the casing. Tie a bow around the two top ends of the dowel and make a wool hanger.

Tree Pillow

Pillows are always fun to make. This design combines patchwork and quilting to form a tree motif. The motif is quilted in a Clam Shell pattern (Fig. 29). The pillow measures 14″ × 14″ complete.

Materials:
½ yard of dotted fabric, 44″ or 45″ wide

¾ yard of flowered fabric, 44″ or 45″ wide

1 yard of solid colored fabric

Cotton batting

Pillow stuffing—either shredded foam or a 14″ × 14″ ready-made pillow

White thread

Each finished square will measure 2″ × 2″. Make a tracing, then a template, from the 2½″ × 2½″ actual size square provided (Fig. 28). These measurements include the ¼″ seam allowance.

You'll need to cut the following amount of squares according to the pattern:

19 squares of dotted fabric

26 squares of flowered fabric

4 squares of solid fabric

To sew the squares together, along the ¼″ seam allowance, work the rows as in Fig. 30.

Tree Pillow

129

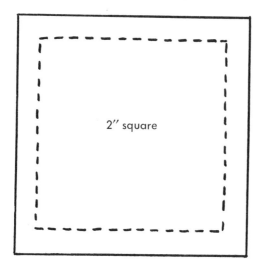

2″ square

Fig. 28

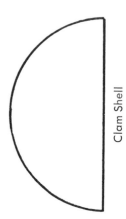

Clam Shell

Fig. 29

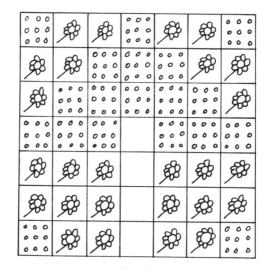

Fig. 30

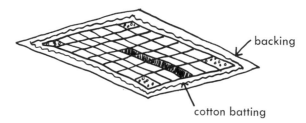

backing

cotton batting

Fig. 31

ROW ONE: One dotted, two flowered, one dotted, two flowered, one dotted.

ROW TWO: Two flowered, three dotted, two flowered. Sew Rows One and Two together.

ROW THREE: One flowered, five dotted, one flowered. Sew Row Three to Row Two.

ROW FOUR: Three dotted, one solid, three dotted. Sew Row Four to Row Three.

ROW FIVE: Three flowered, one solid, three flowered. Sew Row Five to Row Four.

ROW SIX: Three flowered, one solid, three flowered. Sew Row Six to Row Five.

ROW SEVEN: One dotted, two flowered, one solid, two flowered, one dotted. Sew Row Seven to Row Six.

Press seam allowances open.

Cut a piece of solid fabric 18″ × 18″. Overlay it with a piece of cotton batting the same size. Baste together. Place the pillow front on the cotton batting as in Fig. 31. Baste through the three layers with long stitches. Be sure that the seam allowances are lying flat and that there aren't any bumps.

TO QUILT: *All* the dotted squares and the *four solid* squares will be quilted with a Clam Shell pattern. Trace out the pattern (Fig. 29) and make a cardboard template. Place the straight edge of the Clam Shell on the seam lines between rows. Trace the curve only. (See Fig. 32.)

Insert the quilting layers in a quilting hoop. With white thread, quilt the dotted squares with the Clam Shell pattern curve going up, as in Fig. 31, except for three dotted squares on the bottom row which are quilted with the curve facing downwards (Fig. 32). The tree trunk, made up of the four solid squares, is also quilted with the Clam Shell curve in reverse, as shown in Fig. 32.

When all the dotted and solid squares are quilted, remove the pillow front from the quilting hoop. Trim away the excess cotton batting and solid color backing. The pillow should now measure 14½″ × 14½″.

FINISHING: Cut a 14½″ × 14½″ square from the solid color fabric for the backing. Place the *right* side of the pillow front to the *right* side of the solid color backing. Pin. Sew around three sides of the pillow, using a ¼″

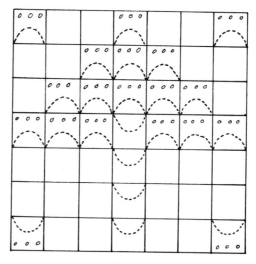

Fig. 32

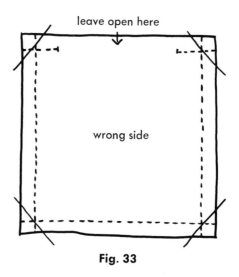

leave open here

wrong side

Fig. 33

seam allowance. Leave about ten inches of the fourth side open so you can easily stuff the pillow (Fig. 33).

Clip the four corners so that when you turn the pillow right side out, the corners will be sharp (Fig. 33).

Turn the pillow right side out. Stuff with shredded foam or a ready-made pillow square. Sew the open ten-inch seam closed with a small hemming stitch.

Bolero

Put the versatility of patchwork to a new use by making your own fabric. Bolero patterns are readily available from sewing pattern companies. Instructions call for a half yard of fabric—and this is what you will make. When you see how simple it is to make your own lengths of patchwork fabric, you'll want to make all or part of this design for a co-ordinating mini-skirt, long pants, or knickers that are usually included with the bolero pattern. Here's how to begin the bolero:

Bolero made from patchwork material

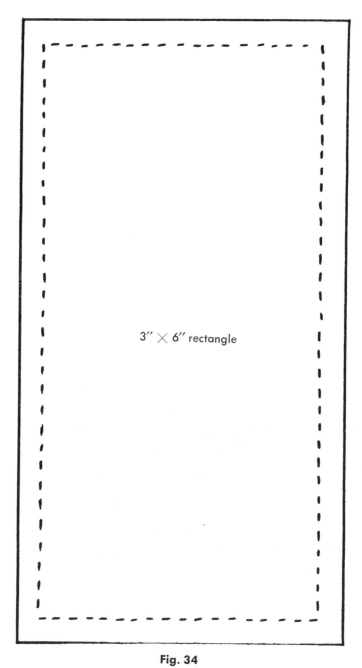

3″ × 6″ rectangle

Fig. 34

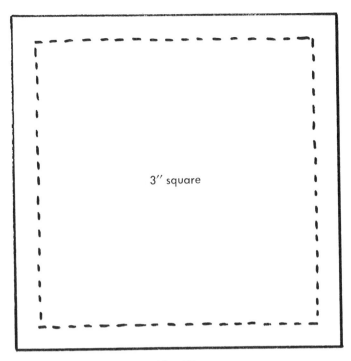

3″ square

Fig. 35

The pattern calls for a half yard of 36″ wide fabric. This means a length of material that will measure one-half yard (18″) by one yard (36″). The pattern for the fabric is made up of three 6″ squares, which add up to the 18″ side, and six 6″ squares, which add up to the 36″ side (Figs. 34, 35).

Materials: You will need five different fabrics—four printed and one solid color. Fig. 36 shows how each square is divided into halves, quarters, or kept in one piece. Fig. 37 shows how the five different fabrics are pieced together. All fabrics should be 44″–45″ wide.

Piece #1—½ yard of printed fabric
Piece #2—½ yard of a different print
Piece #3—⅛ yard of a solid color
Piece #4—⅛ yard of a different print
Piece #5—⅛ yard of a different print
Lining—½ yard of a solid color
Three yards of rickrack in the color of your choice

Thread

Pins and scissors

Measure a 6½″ × 6½″ pattern for the 6″ square. The patterns have been provided for the 3″ square and the rectangle (Figs. 34 and 35). The seam allowance of ¼″ has been indicated on the patterns. Make a template for each piece, and then cut the following amounts of each piece:

Piece #1—cut 18–3″ squares

Piece #2—cut 18–3″ squares

Piece #3—cut 6–6″ squares

Piece #4—cut 3 rectangles

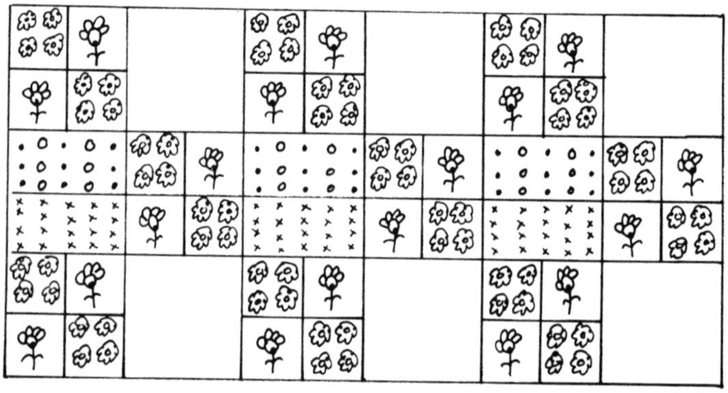

Fig. 36

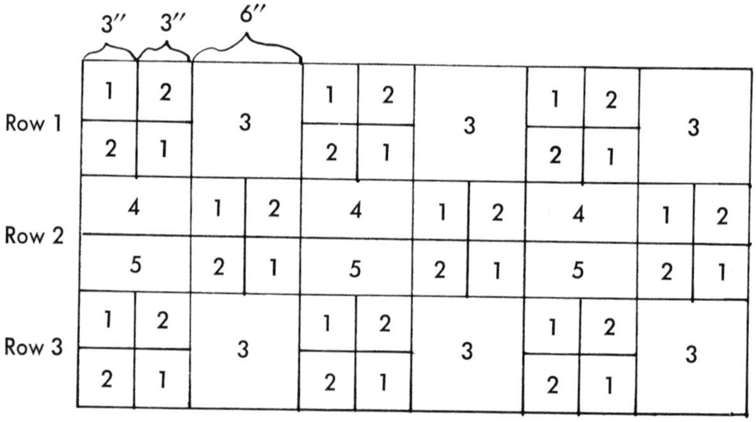

Fig. 37

Piece #5—cut 3 rectangles

ROW ONE: The first 6″ square is a *four-patch* made with contrasting floral prints—*each* piece a 3″ square. To make it, sew #1 to #2, then #2 to #1. Sew the two sections together to make the four-patch (Fig. 37). Make three four-patches. Now, alternate a four-patch with a solid color square—#3 in the diagram—so that you have six 6″ squares, which will complete Row One. Press the seams.

ROW TWO: This row alternates a four-patch (made from #1 and #2) with a two-patch made from contrasting patterns, #4 and #5. Sew #4 to #5, along the 6½″ side. Make three (Fig. 37). Make three more 6″ squares from #1 and #2. Begin the row with the 6″ square made from #4 and #5 rectangles. Alternate with the four-patch until you have six squares, to complete Row Two. Press the seams. Sew Row Two to Row One.

ROW THREE: Row Three is the same as Row One. Complete this row then, after pressing, sew it to Row Two. Press the seam.

Now you're ready to pin the bolero pattern to the patchwork fabric you've made.

Fold the fabric in half lengthwise and pin the bolero sections down according to the directions on the sewing pattern (Fig. 38).

Note: When you cut out the bolero pattern, the patchwork seams will open up slightly as you cut across them. Before you sew the bolero parts together, tack the patches along their seam lines where they became disjoined.

Make the darts in each front, then sew the fronts to the backs with a ⅝″ seam (Fig. 39).

To make a lining, use a solid color material and cut the pattern out identically to the bolero. Sew the lining to the bolero, right sides together, leaving an opening on the bottom so that you can turn it to the right side. Leave the *shoulder seams on the fronts and the back open.* Do not yet sew the lining to the front on the shoulder seams (Fig. 40).

Turn the bolero right side out. To sew the shoulder seams together, sew the *lining only* of the fronts and the back together (Fig. 41).

Now that the lining sections are sewn together, sew the bolero front and back sections together by turning under the seam allowance, then

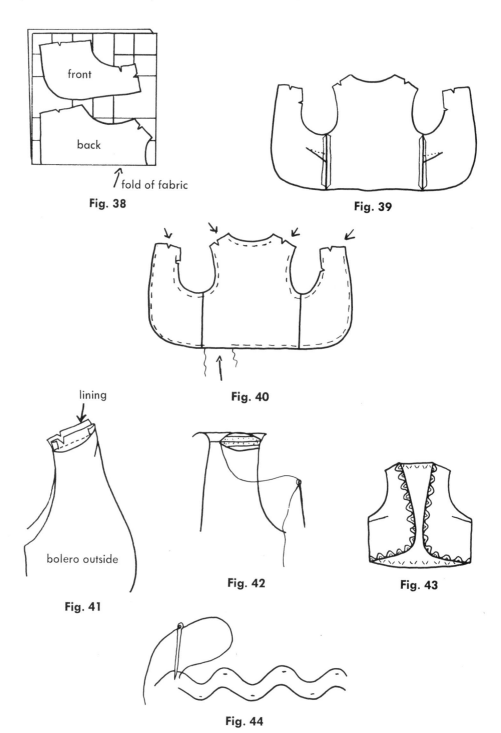

front

back

fold of fabric

Fig. 38

Fig. 39

Fig. 40

lining

bolero outside

Fig. 41

Fig. 42

Fig. 43

Fig. 44

sew together with a hemming stitch (Fig. 42).

Sew rickrack around the edge of the bolero. Begin at the center of the neck edge in back and work around the sides, bottom, up the other side, and join at the starting point (Fig. 43).

To sew the rickrack: Baste the rickrack in place. Use thread to match and take a tiny stitch on the outside tips of each triangular turn of the rickrack, as shown in Fig. 44. This will give you another pattern on the inside of the bolero with the thread. The *long* stitches that will show on the lining make a leaf pattern, while the tiny stitch on the rickrack will barely show.

Log Cabin Quilt

This is a traditional patchwork pattern called the Log Cabin. It's made of squares and rectangles, with a particular scheme that makes it different. One side of the completed block is pieced with dark fabric prints, and the other side with light, as in Fig. 45.

Log Cabin Quilt

139

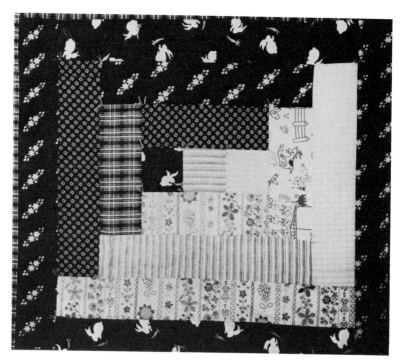

One block of Log Cabin Quilt

This Log Cabin quilt is made up of six large blocks, each block made of fourteen pieces, and the whole bound in a dark plaid. But your choice of color and pattern will determine the color of the binding. The quilting stitch that is used is a *tacking* stitch that's worked on the corners of each piece. The tacking stitch is a technique often used by quiltmakers to join the three layers of a quilt together. You'll find that this is really simple to do.

Materials: Use cotton or cotton mixture fabrics that are 44"–45" wide.
Piece #1—⅛ yard of dark fabric
Piece #2—⅛ yard of light fabric
Piece #3—⅛ yard of light
Piece #4—¼ yard of dark
Piece #5—¼ yard of light
Piece #6—¼ yard of dark
Piece #7—¼ yard of light

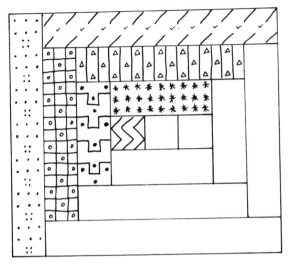

Fig. 45

Piece #8—¼ yard of dark
Piece #9—¼ yard of light
Piece #10—¼ yard of dark
Piece #11—¼ yard of light
Piece #12—½ yard of dark
Piece #13—½ yard of light
Piece #14—½ yard of dark
4 yards of fabric for the backing
1 yard of fabric for the binding
One package of cotton batting
Embroidery floss
Thread

For the patterns, you'll need to make *four* templates, one each, of the following sizes:

3½″ × 3½″ square
3½″ × 9½″ rectangle
3½″ × 15½″ rectangle
3½″ × 21½″ rectangle

These measurements allow for the ¼″ seam allowance all around. When these pieces are sewn together, their finished sizes are: 3″ × 3″; 3″ × 9″; 3″ × 15″; 3″ × 21″.

Cut *six* of *each* piece as follows (see Fig. 46 for the scheme):

For #1—use the 3½″ × 3½″ square template and cut six in a dark patterned fabric.

For #2—use the 3½″ × 3½″ template and cut six light.

For #3—use the 3½″ × 3½″ template and cut six light.

For #4—use the 3½″ × 9½″ template and cut six dark.

For #5—use the 3½″ × 9½″ template and cut six light.

For #6—use the 3½″ × 9½″ template and cut six dark.

For #7—use the 3½″ × 9½″ template and cut six light.

For #8—use the 3½″ × 15½″ template and cut six dark.

For #9—use the 3½″ × 15½″ template and cut six light.

For #10—use the 3½″ × 15½″ template and cut six dark.

For #11—use the 3½″ × 15½″ template and cut six light.

For #12—use the 3½″ × 21½″ template and cut six dark.

For #13—use the 3½″ × 21½″ template and cut six light.

For #14—use the 3½″ × 21½″ template and cut six dark.

Directions for making each block: Fig. 46 shows how the fourteen

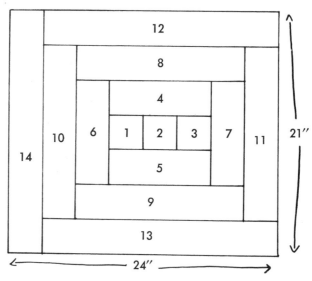

Fig. 46

142

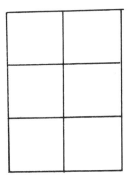

Fig. 47

pieces that make up a block are sewn together. The finished dimensions of each block are 21″ × 24″. Assembly is as follows:

Sew #1 (dark) to #2 (light) as in Fig. 48

Sew #3 (light) to #2 (light) as in Fig. 49

Sew #4 (dark) to the top edge of 1+2+3 as in Fig. 50

Sew #5 (light) to the bottom edge of 1+2+3 as in Fig. 51

Sew #6 (dark) to the left edge of 4+1+5 as in Fig. 52

Sew #7 (light) to the right edge of 4+3+5 as in Fig. 53

Sew #8 (dark) to the top edge of 6+4+7 as in Fig. 54

Sew #9 (light) to the bottom edge of 6+5+7 as in Fig. 55

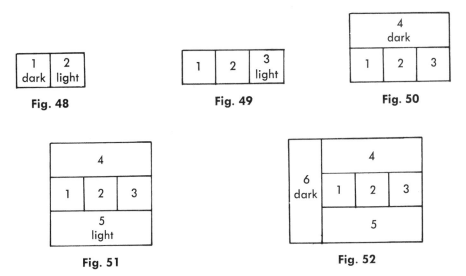

Fig. 48 **Fig. 49** **Fig. 50**

Fig. 51 **Fig. 52**

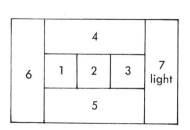

Fig. 53

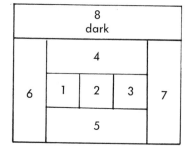

Fig. 54

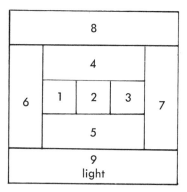

Fig. 55

Sew #10 (dark) to the left edge of 8+6+9 as in Fig. 56

Sew #11 (light) to the right edge of 8+7+9 as in Fig. 57

Sew #12 (dark) to the top edge of 10+8+11 as in Fig. 58

Sew #13 (light) to the bottom edge of 10+9+11 as in Fig. 59

Sew #14 (dark) to the left edge of 12+10+13 as in Fig. 60

This completes the first block. Make five more blocks in the same way. Sew the blocks together, two across and three down, as in Fig. 47.

TO QUILT: The quilting will be done with a tacking stitch. Use either embroidery thread or buttonhole twist in a light color. The tacking stitch will be made on every corner of each section.

First, make the backing. Cut the 4-yard piece of backing into two 2-yard pieces. Each 2-yard piece will measure 72″ long. Cut 4″ off the bottom of each piece so that it measures 68″. Sew the two pieces, right sides together, with a ½″ seam down the 68″ length. With the two pieces still right side to right side, measure 10″ from the edge—*not* the seam edge—and mark with a pencil all the way down the 68″ length, as shown in Fig. 61. Pin the edges and cut through both pieces. This will trim the backing down to 52″ × 68″. (These measurements are for fabric that is 36″ wide. For 45″ wide fabric, take off 19″ after the seam is made. A seam down the *center* makes it neater. If necessary, instead of joining two 45″ pieces and trimming so that the back is symmetrical, add a 7″ × 68″ strip to one 45″ × 68″ piece. This will add up to the correct finished dimensions.)

Press the seam allowance open. Spread the backing on the floor, wrong

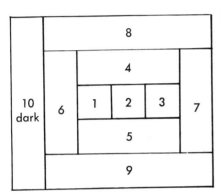

Fig. 56

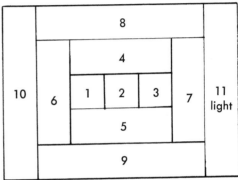

Fig. 57

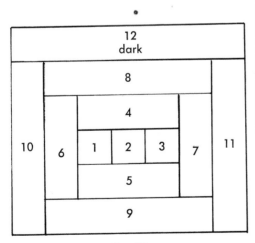

Fig. 58

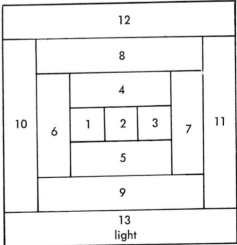

Fig. 59

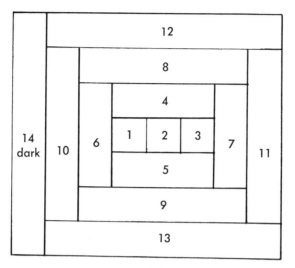

Fig. 60

side up. Unroll the sheet of cotton batting and cover the backing with it. Trim off any excess so that it fits the backing.

Taking long basting stitches, secure the batting onto the backing. Work from the center out, stitching on a diagonal. Keep smoothing the batting so that there aren't any gathers or bumps.

Place the Log Cabin quilt front on the cotton batting. Be sure that the seam allowances are lying flat. With large basting stitches, secure the top of the quilt to the *two* other layers (Fig. 62).

When the basting is completed, you're ready to begin the quilting. Place a portion of each block of the quilt in a quilting hoop or large embroidery hoop. The quilting tack is done block by block. The three layers should be firmly in the hoop, smooth and taut, before tacking.

The Tacking Stitch: Use embroidery thread or buttonhole twist. *Do not make a knot on the end of the thread.* Go in *from the top* and through the three layers at the corner point. Leave about 1½" at the end of the thread. Hold the end of the thread with your thumb so that it doesn't pull through as you take the stitches. Make a tiny stitch from underneath and come out about ¼" away from the start. Pull the thread, but do not pull the 1½" piece through (Fig. 63A). Go back into the first stitch hole and pull through the three layers (Fig. 63B).

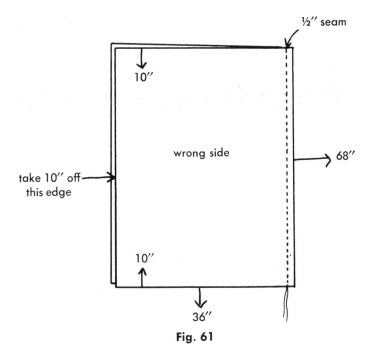

10"

take 10" off
this edge

wrong side

68"

10"

36"

Fig. 61

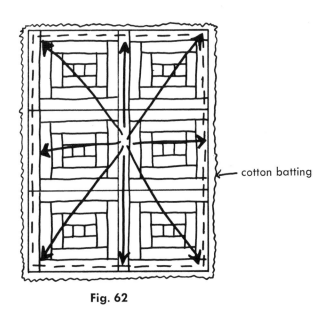

cotton batting

Fig. 62

The needle is now underneath. To make the second half of the stitch, go back up through the second hole, as in Fig. 63B.

Fig. 63A

Fig. 63B

Fig. 63C

Fig. 64

Pull to tighten. Clip the end of the thread so that there are two loose ends standing up, as in Fig. 63C. The stitch is now completed.

Make a tacking stitch on each corner of each piece in each block. When all the stitches are done, trim them so that they are all the same length.

FINISHING: When the tacking is all completed, keep the long basting stitches on the quilt and trim the excess cotton batting and backing off (Fig. 64). Trim all four sides.

To sew on the binding, cut strips for the binding in the following sizes:

One piece—1½″ wide × 48½″ long

One piece—1½″ wide × 64¾″ long

One piece—1½″ wide × 49½″ long

One piece—1½″ wide × 65½″ long

Sew the binding strips on in the following order: Pin the 48½″ long

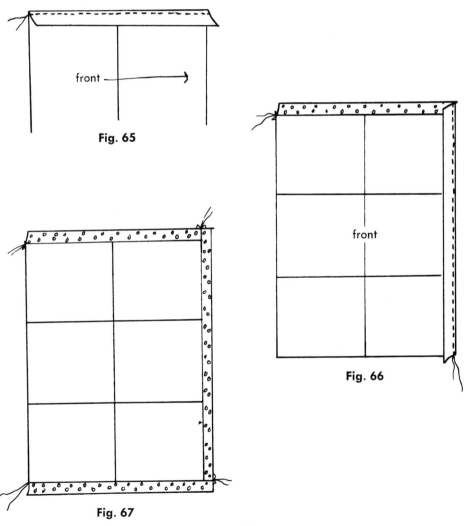

front

Fig. 65

front

Fig. 66

Fig. 67

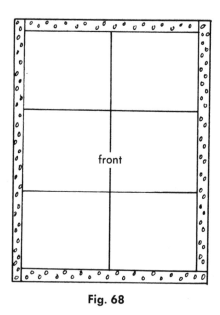

Fig. 68

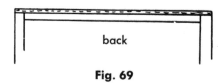

back

Fig. 69

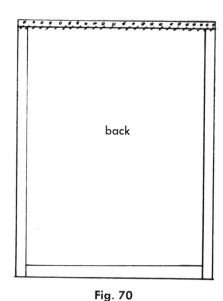

back

Fig. 70

strip to the *top* edge. Be sure that you pin the binding to the front of the quilt—*right sides* together. Baste. Sew across the top with a ¼″ seam allowance (Fig. 65).

To sew the binding to the *right edge* of the quilt, first lift up the top edge binding as shown in Fig. 66. Pin the right edge piece, which is 64¾″ long, to the top edge of the piece and the length of the quilt. Baste. Sew along the ¼″ seam allowance.

The third strip, which is 49½″ long and goes across the bottom edge of the quilt, is sewn in the same manner. Lift open the side edge binding strip and attach the bottom strip all along the open strip and the bottom edge of the quilt. It will look like Fig. 67 when the three sides are open.

The fourth strip is 65½″ long and is attached to the open binding edges of the bottom and top. Pin. Baste in place. Sew with a ¼″ seam allowance. Fig. 68 shows the four open strips of binding.

On the back, turn down a ¼″ hem on the edges of the strips as shown in Fig. 69. Baste the ¼″ hem allowance all around the four strips. Now your binding should measure 1″ wide.

Fold down the binding on the back and align it with the seam lines on the back. Pin and baste. Sew the binding down with a hemming stitch. The binding will measure ½″ wide in the front and ½″ wide on the back (Fig. 70).

Crazy Quilting Pillow

Crazy quilting has always been one of those fun ways to make a quilt, since it's done thoroughly by improvisation. If you like the odd shapes of scraps and do not like to work in a very precise way all the time, crazy quilting is a nice, loose form to try. Originally the crazy quilt was a true example of using fabric scraps, no matter what their texture, color, or size.

Crazy-quilt Pillow

151

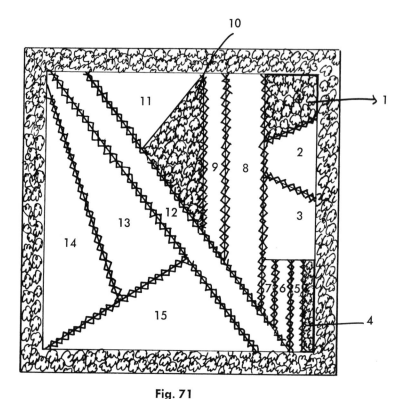

Fig. 71

The quilt was built up random piece by random piece. Often, decorative stitches added along the seams and on the scraps themselves gave the needle-woman a great sense of pride in her skills at quilting. Eventually, in the late 1800's, the crazy quilt was given a new status—velvet and silk scraps replaced gingham and sturdy woolens. Embroidery stitches became an essential part of the design.

This crazy quilt pillow is a newer interpretation, since it's not done in the traditional way. The traditional way is to set each piece on an already padded foundation piece of muslin or fine cotton, adding and trimming the pieces one by one. This crazy quilt pattern has been worked out more like a patchwork. Simple geometric shapes were pieced together. All the pieces were laid down to see which sides would all work together in groups for sewing. The pieces were trimmed here and there before sewing so that each piece would be a perfect fit for the other.

The pieces were sewn together in groups, then the groups sewn together (Fig. 71).

Pieces 1+2+3 were sewn to each other first, then put aside.

Pieces 4+5+6+7 were sewn together, then both groups were seamed together along the bottom edge of piece 3.

Pieces 8+9+10+11 were sewn together. Piece 8's right edge attached this group to the long side edge that includes, going vertically, 1+2+3+7.

Piece 12 was sewn along the edges of pieces 11+10+9+8+7+6.

Pieces 13+14 were sewn together, then attached to piece 15. These three pieces were sewn to the left edge of piece 12.

After the seam allowances were pressed, the front was embroidered with a cross-stitch along every seam line. The border of flowered material was sewn around the four sides. A back was made, sewn to the front, and the pillow was stuffed.

INDEX

THE AUTHOR

Constance Bogen has written for several magazines and is the author of a recent adult book on macrame. A native New Yorker, she travels extensively and loves to collect unusual needlework.